ROBERT E. AND AGNES JUST REID
A Historical Collection

By Merle Reid Clark

ISBN: 978-1-7341924-6-9
Published by Cedar Creek Press, Boise, Idaho
Copyright 2024 by Merle Reid Clark

Table of Contents

Introduction 3
Robert Reid Family Tree 6
Robert's Paternal Great Grandparents 8
   James and Jane Gray Millar 8
   Richard and Marjory (May) Rendall Reid 10
Robert's Paternal Grandparents 11
   James Edward and Jean Reid Miller 11
      Mount Pleasant 16
Robert's Maternal Great Grandparents 19
   Samuel Thadmore and Anna Jemima Loughery Bell 19
Robert's Maternal Grandparents 22
   Andrew and Mary Ellen Bell Goodenough 22
Robert's Parents 27
   James (Gam) and Isabell Goodenough Reid 27
      Letters from Gam 32
Robert E. Reid and Agnes Just Reid 51
   Children of Robert and Agnes 56
   Eldro Just (El) Reid 56
   Robert Vincent 63
   Fred Bennett 68
   Douglass James 73
   Wallace Richard 76
Grandy 79
Mimi 83
   Mimi's Writings 84
      Poetry 84
      Good Reviews and Rejections 87
      Correspondence 87
      Columns 90
      Letters of Long Ago 91
   Mimi's Philosophy 93
The Young Reid Boys in the Old House 95
Mimi and Grandy in Their Later Years 106
Neighbors, Friends, and Origins of Reid Sayings 115
Critters 123
Machinery and Vehicles 127
Burial Sites 130
Epilogue 130
Sources 131

Introduction

I have always been interested in history, especially my Reid side. Since my Dad and his brothers were such wonderful men, gentle, handsome, honorable, and funny, I knew our grandfather Robert had to be the same. Though he died before most of his grandchildren were born, we all felt a connection to him and lovingly called him the name he was known by in the family, Grandy. I wrote a book about my Grandmother Agnes's ancestors, both her maternal Thompson side and her paternal Just side. This book is about her husband, my grandfather, Robert Ezekiel Reid, his ancestors and his five sons. I wanted his descendants to know how wonderful he was, and how special his family was that gave love so freely. What a legacy!

When my Uncle Doug Reid died, he left the ancestral home to the Presto Preservation Association, which had been created in 1994 by the descendants of Nels and Emma Just. The home was placed on the National Register of Historic places in 2020 and is currently being lovingly restored. Most of the book is information found at this old house. Mimi, our name for our grandma Agnes, was a writer, most notably of *Letters of Long Ago*, but also of poems and prose, and she had a wide correspondence with many friends and family. She kept carbon copies of many of these letters, and some were returned to her after many years had gone by. Nelle Vincent, her good friend, and Ursell Hutchinson Bennett, Jack Bennett's wife, both did this.

For my purposes, quotes are italicized and the author's name enclosed in parentheses. I wanted this book to be as near to the truth as possible. Luckily Mimi shared stories about their lives, important or mundane. Their family love is evident in her words. We are blessed that the house was left vacant for so long and that Doug and Mimi were self-confessed hoarders because it has been a treasure trove of historical documents and objects.

(Mimi wrote) *Doug and I hoard everything.* We found that to be true. After Doug died, we nieces went through Kittie Reid Blair's house where Doug lived as her caregiver for many years. It was full of objects most people would consider junk.

I asked questions of my other uncles, Wallace and Vin, and their wives, Gwen and Marlene. These women were both historians in their own right. Gwen was in the family when Grandy was alive, so she had some firsthand information. I spent lots of time with my Dad, Fred Reid, and Uncle Doug in their later years. I peppered them with questions about growing-up and what they remembered of stories handed down.

I have compiled all of this information under headings of who was being talked about, or of subjects in common.

Some family stories have been disproven by written documents uncovered. I believe the document over a memory. But even so, there must have been a grain of truth to get the stories started and it's fun to see how far some of these stories are from the documentation. I have noted the discrepancy.

The census is my favorite tool. America takes a census every 10 years on the decade, as in 1900. England, Scotland and Canada take it every 10 years the year after, as in 1901. Before 1850 they weren't very informative, but afterwards there is a plethora of information on each household. It is a snapshot of who lives in that house on that date. The 1890 census was destroyed in a fire, which leaves a very big hole in the information during those 20 years. In the latest census of 2020, in which I participated, we have reverted to a minimum of information collected once again.

I kept a genealogy tree with both my Mom and Dad's ancestors. When the Presto Preservation Association got a membership to Ancestry.com, I entered all my information. It is a wonderful site. Every person has a page which can hold photos, stories and documents, starting with birth records and ending with a death certificate and burial place. These can include everything that records a person's life, every time a person wrote his name, immigration and military records, censuses, or what is written about them in a newspaper. I have heard from people all over the U. S. and England and Scotland, who share a common ancestor with me. You can save something from someone else's tree to your own tree. They may have a tidbit of information we didn't know or a photo we haven't seen.

An example of this wonderful benefit is Grandy's grandfather, Sam Bell. A Bell descendant had submitted a picture with a typewritten notation on the bottom, "one of the Bells." I think it has to be our Sam because his wife is in the same setting in the photo we had, and they look to be the same age. Like many of the things found, it will probably never be known for sure. I had a picture that I know is Sam but he is old and the picture is blurry. If you can connect a photo to a name, it is much easier to keep them straight in your mind.

I urge you to go to ancestry.com and look up our wonderful Just/Reid tree. I have done the genealogy as well as I can, but it's a leap of faith to believe that it's completely correct. As more information becomes available, it may be changed - or more likely, will never be known for sure. Some family lines reach back for many generations, hundreds of years. Some family lines stop with a first name just a few short generations ago.

The LDS Church has many members working to find records, which affords an advantage to members, old and new. If an ancestor emigrated as a Mormon convert, or had been in America for generations before joining the church, there is lots of information. Both the Bells and Goodenoughs were Mormon converts, but were later excommunicated. There is not much information about their ancestral lines. Lots of questions, not many answers.

I made a timeline that is currently on display in the Just/Reid home. It shows events in different families, historic happenings, and improvements in the old house. It shows a square for each year from 1800 to 2020. Each year in the decade reads from left to right, 1801, 1802, etc. The decades read down vertically. Each family or category is in a different color. The Thompson line finishes with George Thompson's death. Emma

Thompson goes from being in the Thompson line, then the Bennett line, and finally to the Just line, as she married. It looks overwhelming, but as long as you follow these guidelines it is fun and easy. Each family's line is in each year square. For example, Emma Thompson is born the same year in England, 1850, as James Reid (Robert's dad) in Scotland. The house history notes important things like when the house got indoor plumbing, or fun to know trivia, like the daisy linoleum installation, and recent restoration for the year it happened. There is also a color for historic events like the sinking of the Titanic.

In this book I have noted our genealogy line with a star and bolded the name of the child. It will help the reader to refer back to the genealogy tree.

Since our Miller/Reid line has so many individuals named James, I have designated them to make it easier to keep them straight. James Millar (with an "a") never left the Island of Westray. His son, James Edward Miller (with an "e") went back and forth. His son, James Miller Reid, who I'll call "Gam," took his mother's maiden name. His son is my grandfather, Robert. Robert's brother is also named James but went by Jim.

JAMES - EACH LINE IS A GENERATION

James Millar - buried on Westray, Orkney Islands

James Edward Miller – went to America, then back to Scotland, came back to America and died here

James (Miller) Reid - "Gam"   - father to Robert

James Edward Reid - (Jim)   - brother to Robert

Robert Reid's father, James Miller, took his mother's maiden name of Reid. There is no information about why he would have done this.

My dad is Fred, son of Robert and Agnes Reid. My mother is Alma Jemmett Reid. Of course the memories and pictures are more plentiful on my side, but all memories were similar and all the brothers were loved equally.

Agnes Just Reid is Mimi to everyone in the Reid family and I use this name throughout my writing.

Robert E. Reid is also known as Bob, R. E., Rufus, Zeke, and the name his grandkids gave him and most familiar to me, Grandy.

6

Robert Reid Family Tree

GREAT GRANDPARENTS
James Millar

GRANDPARENTS
James Edward Miller

Jane Gray

DAD
James Miller Reid (Gam)

Richard Reid

Margaret (Jean) Reid

Marjory (May) Rendall

Robert Reid

GREAT GRANDPARENTS
Erastus Goodenough

GRAND PARENTS
John Andrew Goodenough

Marie C.

MOM
Isabell Goodenough

Samuel Thadmore Bell

Mary Ellen Bell

Anna Jemima Watson Loughery

Robert's Paternal Great Grandparents

The Millers and Reids came from the Orkney Islands situated miles off the northeast tip of mainland Scotland. The biggest island is Orkney and there are 67 islands in the chain.

Our Miller and Reid ancestors lived on the island of Westray for generations. My sisters and I took a "trip of a lifetime" to England and Scotland in 2014. We flew into London, then worked our way north on the train to the top of mainland Scotland. We rented a van and drove it onto a ferry going to the Orkney Islands. To get there, we had to take two ferries and it took one and a half hours. We relished the ocean and ferry ride. We could see an island approaching in the distance and finally see it disappear behind us. Some of the islands aren't inhabited. Westray and Papa Westray are the farthest northern islands. Westray is small with two main villages and a six-mile lane to connect them. It was the favorite part of our trip.

I wondered about these people, our ancestors, coming from an island with the sea crashing against the shores; a place far enough north that they spent months in darkness in the winter. Westray is small and isolated so I'm sure everyone knew each other. To bring a wife and 10 children across the sea, knowing you may never be back to see loved ones, to make new friends and start over; I am in awe that they had the courage to do that.

James and Jane Gray Millar
Lady Kirk Graveyard

James Millar　　　　　　　　　　**Jane Gray Millar**
1790 - Dec 15, 1830　　　　　March 31, 1789 - Jan 22, 1879

We saw the headstone that James Edward Miller erected for his mother and father. They used an "a" instead of an "e" which is how it was spelled for successive generations. I can't explain why it was changed. I've found the practice of changing the spelling of surnames to be common in my research. James and Jane had 6 children. Our James was the only boy and was 5 yrs old when his father, age 40, was killed in a shipwreck on the River Tees in northern England.

The Lady Kirk graveyard is right on the ocean shore, and very close to the Mount Pleasant House you will read about later.

We learned this story about the graveyard: There was a long and fierce storm that lasted several days. It covered the graves with sand up to six feet deep. It was impossible to uncover the graves, so they started burying people on top of the older graves. Luckily our ancestors were in the latter section. The church floor is several feet below ground because the sand drifted up to the windows.

Children

Margaret Trail	1818
Mary	1820 - 1844
Jean	1821
Isabella	Dec 29, 1823 - April 29, 1872
*James Edward	**July 13, 1825 - 26 Dec, 1913**
Ann	1829 – 1891

I found a neat story about Isabella. She married James Logie in Scotland. They came to America around the horn of South America, stopped at Hawaii to trade, then settled in Oregon on an island. There Isabell was much loved by the Indians as a healer. She brought medicinal plants from Scotland and planted them in Oregon to use. James died in Oregon. They had no children. Her second husband was Johnathan Moar. They were parents of 5 children. Isabell died at 49.

Richard and Marjory (May) Rendall Reid
Lady Kirk Graveyard

Richard Reid
March 25, 1806 - Nov 21, 1897

Marjory (May) Rendall Reid
about 1808 – May 28, 1891

Children

*Margaret (Jean)	March 30, 1827 - Aug 8, 1872
Ann	1830
Robert	1833 - Feb 25, 1870
May	1837
John David	1839 - 1901
Jean	1841
James	1844 - Feb 18, 1922
Thomas	1848 - Dec 5, 1876

I don't know much about this family. I was tickled to find in a census in 1861, that one of James and Margaret Millar's daughters, Jemima, 9, was staying with her grandparents Richard and May Reid.

I don't think any of the family except Margaret (Jean) came to America.

Robert's Paternal Grandparents

James Edward and Jean Reid Miller

James Edward Miller
July 13, 1825 - Dec 26, 1913

(no picture)
Jean Reid Miller
March 30, 1827 - Aug 8, 1872

Children

Marjory (Mae)	1848 – 1930
*James Miller (Reid) (Gam)	March 3, 1850 - Jan 15, 1936
Jemima (Mymie)	1852 – after 1930
Margaretta (Maggie)	1854 – 1937
Betsy	1856 – 1900
Richard	1858 – 1875
Robert (unmarried)	1860 - after 1875
Jean (Jennie)	1862 – 1942
Isabella (Belle)	1865 – 1903
Mary	1867 -

    James is a very common name. I had an awful time trying to keep another James Miller from our tree. I had a census of 1871 In Scotland, a census in America for 1870, a passenger list for 1872, and Jean dying in America a few months after they arrived. They couldn't all be right. Although I haven't found any passenger list for our ancestors, they were recorded on a census question as coming to America in 1869.

    James and Jean had 10 children. They would have come to America after 1867 as the youngest daughter was born in Scotland. The census for 1870 has everyone, parents and 9 kids, living in Providence, Rhode Island, USA, all but Mae. Jean is there then and our James (Gam) is there, still a Miller. Jean died in 1872, and is buried in Rhode Island, so not in the 1880 census. James Miller, who had taken his mother's maiden name of Reid, was in Idaho. James Edward Miller married again to Jane McKay. They returned to Scotland where they lived on the island of Westray and are in the 1891 and 1901 censuses in Scotland. They returned to America, probably with Isabella after her visit to the island, and in the 1910 census were living in Rhode Island. They are living near widowed Mae and her family. James Edward Miller died in Rhode Island in 1913.

(Mimi wrote, in a letter to Bessie, granddaughter of James Edward Miller*) Father Reid (Gam) once told me that his father not only sang but composed music, so that had to be musical. Two of the other boys did some fiddling but my husband just used his divine voice.*

Children of James Edward and Jean Reid Miller

Marjory (Mae) **Cusiter** (Custer) Married James Cusiter. She was married in Scotland and came to America separate from her family, but probably about the same time. Their first child was born in Nova Scotia in 1869, but by the 1870 census they are in Rhode Island and all following children were born there. In all the U. S. censuses, the last name is listed as Custer. James Custer died between the 1880 census and 1900.

James (Gam) **Miller Reid**
March 3, 1850 - Jan 15, 1936

Jemima (Mymie) **Miller**
Feb 27, 1852 - after 1930
Married George Miller

Margaretta (Maggie) Cameron
March 23, 1854 - 1937
Married Herbert Cameron. They had a daughter named Ethel.

Ethel Cameron   Mimi, Robert and Ethel   Ethel in Robert's chaps

(Gwen wrote) *Ethel Cameron was Robert's cousin from Providence, Rhode Island, who came to the Reid Ranch to visit "Cousin Rob." We all adored her. She had never married, but was certainly an 'unforgettable character.' She was ready for anything and everything."* Fred remembered Ethel sending presents before she came. Gwen kept up a correspondence for the rest of Ethel's life. She died in 1960 at 83.

(Mimi wrote) *She (Ethel) took Kit and me as far as Salt Lake and kept us a week, paying all expenses. We had a good time and we enjoyed having her here for so long but I have neglected all my other friends shamefully. Three months is a long time to give to one friend when there are so many others you love and want to see.*

Betsy (McKechnie)
May 2, 1856 – 1900
Married John McKechnie, they had a daughter Bessie.

Bessie McKechnie

Bessie and Nellie Reid (Jim Reid's daughter) corresponded. Nellie gave these pictures and the following letters to Gwen. We are so blessed to have them.

Richard
April 11, 1858 - after 1875
Unmarried, killed railroad collision in Montana

Robert
Oct 9, 1860 - after 1875
Unmarried

Jean (Jennie)
Dec 14, 1862 – April 25, 1942

Isabella (Belle)
June 4, 1865 - April 28, 1903
Married David Howat

Mary
June 7, 1867 –

Most, if not all, of James Reid's sisters settled in Rhode Island, married and had their own households. The brothers never married nor had children. As far as I know none of the family saw James after he came west.

Bessie's Letter to Nellie Reid, daughter of Jim Reid (Robert's brother):
My grandfather, your great Grandfather James Miller, was living 'ay up North in the Orkney Islands of Scotland. He was a very fine, six feet tall, broad shouldered, sternly religious Scotch Presbyterian gentleman. He had a farm there and raised sheep and cattle. The family all helped, the girls worked in the fields as well as the boys. Water for the crops was carried in buckets from a well. Life was not easy for them. And yet there was a light side too. Grandpa had a fine singing voice (That wasn't hear say, I can vouch for it). He had organized and directed a choral group which must have been lots of fun. Evidently it wasn't all hymn-singing as Mother, who probably attended the rehearsals, knew so many lovely songs and Gilbert and Sullivan Operettas.

Grandpa's first wife was Jean Reid. She must have been a saintly woman; Mother always spoke of her with reverence. She was the mother of ten children, seven of which were girls, Marjory (Mae), Jemima (Maymie), Margaretta (Maggie, Ethel's mother), Betsy (Bessie's mother), Jean (Jennie), Isabella (Belle), Mary, James, Robert, Richard.

Grandpa was about 42 years old when he came to America. I don't know whether he brought the whole family with him when he came or whether there were some already here. Some of them attended school here. Don't know how long he stayed or why he returned to Scotland but along about 1900, (I was 13 years old) Aunt Bell decided to go to Scotland to visit them and brought them back to live with her. They seemed very old to me- must have been in their 80's. Grandpa was well in his nineties when he died.

Now then here's where things and I are somewhat mixed up. Your grandfather Reid, (James) was born either before or next after Aunt Mae, Mother spoke of him as being a "fine upright man". Why he adopted his mother's name was unexplained to me, maybe because I wasn't interested enough to ask why. Anyhow he must have had perfectly good reason for doing so else Grandpa Millar would never have sanctioned it. <u>That I Do Know!</u> And James Reid kept his mother's name unblemished.

Richard another son was killed in a railroad accident. He was quite young, wasn't married. Don't know where he fitted in the list - possibly after mother.

With Robert, born after Aunt Jennie, we round out the list of ten children. Robert wasn't married but if ever a man needed a wife, it was poor uncle Bob! He drifted through life always working on a farm and he worked hard......

Mount Pleasant
Pierowall, Westray, Orkney Islands

This is a picture of James Edward Miller and his second wife, Jane, after they moved back to Scotland. James built this house. The second picture is of the same house with my sisters, Janene, Donna, and Kittie standing next to me in front. We knew when we traveled to the Orkney Islands that we wanted to try and find the house, but didn't expect it to be so easy! James had described the house in detail in letters to America. The homes there are made of rock and since they are around a long time, are named. Our Miller house had the lovely name of Mount Pleasant!

Under the ground are flat rocks stacked like slices of bread. There are no trees on the island; if a tree is planted it soon runs into rocks so it isn't stable and ultimately can't survive. All wood is hauled from somewhere else or drifts in from the ocean. Rock is a cheap and enduring building choice. This Mount Pleasant house had been added onto the side but this was the original side. It was very close to the ocean in the center of the little town of Pierowall.

Bessie's letter about the picture (above) of the Mount Pleasant house with James and his wife in Pierowall, Westray, Orkney, Scotland:

This must be after they moved back to the Orkney Islands. I'm looking that address up in the map I am convinced that they were as far away as they could get and still be in Scotland. The picture is most interesting, I think and has a tendency to stir faint emotions Grandfather holding his hat, the lady's gown which seems to be equipped with a train, the little dog whose head appears behind the wall back of Grandfathers right ear and whose job it was to watch over the sheep and keep them from straying? And are those daisies on the "lawn"? What or who is in the shadow in the door way?"

Letters from James Edward Miller

Letter to our James, from James Edward Miller
during his time back in Pierowall, Westray

We have got our house finished I will give you a description of it, It is 26 feet long by 15 inside. We have 10 feet by 15 for our kitchen, then we have 8 feet by 6 for two beds. At the foot of the beds we have 8 feet by 3 for a clothes closet then we have a passage leading into a store room which is 8 feet by 4 of a store room for all our eatables and other things separated from that by a partition. We have a room 8 feet by 11 with a passage from the front door 3 feet or a little more, then we come to the back door we open in to a porch 6 feet square. On the right is a water tank with a facet to draw the water through. On the left is a coal house passing through to the left is our potato bin then we open another door we have our hen house so you see we have not much to go out for in a cold winter's day. We have an acre of ground and I am now busy in fencing it round to keep the sheep and cattle out of it. I have got it all paid for and we have a comfortable home. I expect to be able to do some work this summer if God spares me but there is nothing to do here only the fishing. I am a great deal better since I left America. I have gain 21 lbs. I weigh now 173 lbs. Mother sends her kind love to you all hoping you ? Belle come to Orkney and see us and take one of the little boys with you.

Letter Dec 12, 1896 from Periowall, Westray, Orkney, Scotland. It has to be from James Miller though it isn't signed. The sentences run on with very few periods, or capitalization, but the penmanship is beautiful.

Dear Children we received your very welcome pictures a week after we received your letter but we knew who the pictures was as soon as we got it and more especially by little Richard he is the very picture of the family we could not mistake him we are very glad that you chose such a nice respectable woman for a wife and she is good looking too so we hope that you are kind and loving to her and not let her go to work in the tangles as you have seen your mother obliged to do when you were all young you remember that don't you that was hard times I hope you are not and will never will have such hardship in raising your family you are in a county where there is plenty of bread (this is evidence that they traveled to America looking for a better life) *no doubt you have your troubles anxieties and there is always that in the world where ever we are placed and it is needful for us that it should be to (?) our hearts from it remember this is not our home let us earnestly seek for that Heavenly Home where all these troubles and anxieties are forever gone where we shall enjoy perfect peace and joy and love and be forever happy and are glad the boys are all going to school. They will be growing big fellows now I hope that they are good boys and obedient and always ready to help Father and Mother you surely have a church and Sunday school there, don't you? Go and take them along with you and get their minds filled with the Gospel of truth the word of God while they are still young and they will not forget it when they get old. You will send little Katie over here we need a little girl now to run our errands as we are getting tired and ourselves and she will be great company or yet send us that fine baby in the picture but she would get married here and we would soon lose her perhaps she is engaged and won't come the surest they would be to give us Katie well the Robert Miller you saw in the paper was not ours or we surely would have heard of it we had a letter from? date Sept 30th and they were all well then. Mays next oldest girl Jeanie is dead May has had a great deal of trouble since we left James her husband and four of her children has died she has four left yet three boys and a girl the oldest boy and a girl is able to work the others are young it was her oldest girl that ? ? one a child of two years the other three was from 18 to 24 years old, you ought to write May I have not her address presently she has moved since address to Isa care and she will get it the rest is well as far as we know. Jeanie had a very bad spell of sickness last winter she was some better when she wrote your relations here are all in their usual way. Mother sends her love to you all and very proud of our daughter and the rest of the? thinks that you have chosen a very good wife we remain your affectingly Father and Mother be sure and write soon. You never let us know what you are doing and how you are situated tell us what law you have and what cattle you and what rent you pay and what your house cost a building and all these things you need not to the least backward in lettering no know I sent you some little books let me know if you get them and I will send you some more and get the children to read them and read them carefully yourselves.*

Robert's Maternal Great Grandparents

Samuel Thadmore and Anna Jemima Loughery Bell

Samuel Thadmore Bell
Feb 2, 1814 - April 22, 1896

Anna Jemima Loughery Bell
Dec 9, 1816 - Dec 3, 1901

Children

Roseanne	Feb 19, 1836 - 1856	born in New York
Charles	July 1, 1837	born in New York
Samuel	Nov 8, 1839 - Sep 16, 1844	born in Nauvoo, Ill
Henry James	Jun 7, 1841 - Oct 12, 1928	born in Ontario, Canada
Thadmore	Mar 7, 1843 - 1853	born in Nauvoo, Ill
*Mary Ellen	Aug 28, 1844 – June 18, 1921	born in Nauvoo, Ill
John Franklin	Sep 12, 1847 – June 27, 1932	born in Rock Island, Ill
Joseph	Sept 9, 1849	born in Rock Island, Ill
Robert Bruce	Mar 12, 1852 - Feb 18, 1926	born in Iowa
William Wallis	Jul 17, 1859 - before 1860	born in Utah territory

I'm sure the woman in the photos above is Anna. I think the man is Samuel, but the photo was identified only as "one of the Bells." They look to be about the same age and the settings are the same. They must be husband and wife. This is one of the wonderful things about ancestry.com. People put things on their tree and anyone can save a picture or story or document on their own tree.

Anna Jemima Watson Loughery was born in Johnstown, Montgomery County, New York. Her parents were Charles Loughery and Catherine (unknown last name).

Sam and Anna were married Feb 20, 1836, in New York. They were baptized into the Mormon faith, year unknown. There is a patriarchal blessing July 7, 1845, and an endowment date of Jan 30, 1846, both in Nauvoo, Illinois. Samuel was excommunicated sometime after he came west.

Sam was thought to be a mason of the Mormon temple in Nauvoo. Later occupations were farmer, rancher. In 1850 the family was living in Iowa.

They traveled west from Keokuk, Iowa, with the Cyrus H. Wheelock Company. Departed June 3, 1853, and arrived in Salt Lake City on Oct 10, 1853. There were 447 people including Samuel 39, Ann 37, Rosanna 17, Charles 16, Henry 12, Mary Ellen 8, John Franklin 6, Joseph 4, (Thadmore 10, died either before they left or after their journey).

Mary Ellen, the child in our line, was baptized in Salt Lake City, November 13, 1853.

There is an 1860 census of Samuel Bell living in Jacks Valley, Carson County, Utah. This land is now Nevada, close to Carson City and Reno. They had a cattle ranch in Jack's Valley, just north of Genoa, where they provisioned wagon trains going over the mountains to California. The Bell property was on the Carson River. They were listed as Samuel 44, rancher, born in Ireland. Ann 40, children, (Roseanna missing, was probably married) Charles 22 miner, Henry 18, Mary 14, John 13, Joseph 11, Robert Bruce 9 born in Iowa, and girl, Maria "Indian" 7 born in Utah. The Pony Express had a station in the area and was started the same year, 1860, as the census.

In 1862 the Bells were living in Dayton, Nevada. In 1879, they lived in Idaho.

It is speculated that when Brigham Young called the faithful home to Salt Lake City, the Bells refused to go.

We have this story about the oldest child, Roseanne. She was married to a Dr. Vale. The family story has them dissatisfied with the LDS faith because of polygamy. Supposedly they were on a train going back east. Some Mormon men dressed as Indians took them off the train and they were never seen again. I can find no proof of the story, but she thereafter disappeared from the records. We found a handwritten note in the old house by James Reid that referred to this same incident.

Another family story was told to me by my aunt Gwen of one of Samuel's sons, not sure which one, and his mysterious disappearance as he was on his way to California. He made it past American Falls and as far as "Register Rock" close to Raft River and was never seen again. Nothing was ever recovered of the team, wagon, and the $1,000 he was carrying.

The following is another version I found on ancestry.com. The author is a descendent of the man in question. It adds a different twist to the story. *As to my great-grandfather, yes, he was traveling between my grandmother's ranch in the California high desert and her sister Kate's place in Butte, Montana when he disappeared. My grandmother was always sure he was bushwhacked. But she did have a letter which I now have, from a bartender in Pocatello that says he heard John died in the flu epidemic. Of course, we'll never know for sure. My grandmother was always naturally upset about it.*

Another family story involves the death of Samuel Bell in 1896.

(Gwen wrote) *Grandfather Sam Bell and his wife Ann did not live together a lot of the time. Sam lived with the Goodenoughs* (his daughter Mary Ellen's family) *in Marsh Valley. Ann lived in Pocatello with her brother and two daughters. Sam, his son* (must be grandson 12-year-old Ben) *Ben, Kit and Sam's little dog were traveling in a wagon from Marsh Valley to Pocatello for a visit with Ann. When they reached about where Inkom is today, Sam had a heart attack and toppled off the wagon dead. Ben unhitched the horses and rode one back home to get help. Aunt Kit stayed with the wagon.*

The granddaughter, Kittie, would have been 2 yrs old at the time of the accident. The thought of her staying with her dead grandpa as her uncle rode for help is dreadful, but he did what he thought he had to do. The story is reported quite differently as follows:

May 2, 1896 THE CALDWELL TRIBUNE
CALDWELL IDAHO

An aged man named Samuel Bell was thrown from a wagon and instantly killed near McCammon Wednesday afternoon. He was driving with his daughter Mrs. Goodenough when the wagon struck a chuck hole and threw the old man out killing him instantly. Mr. Bell was 84 years old -Pocatello Tribune.

Why these two versions differ so much is a mystery. Do we believe Gwen? She knew Kittie very well throughout her married life. Or do we believe a reporter for the Caldwell paper?

Ann died in McCammon, Bannock County, Idaho. I saw something about Ann and Samuel being buried nearby in the Robin Cemetery, but I can't find it again so it isn't confirmed. I talked to the caretaker of the Robin cemetery. He couldn't give me any information. He said there is an old part of the cemetery but he doesn't know who is buried there and would love to know.

Robert's Maternal Grandparents

Andrew and Mary Ellen Bell Goodenough

Andrew Goodenough
Nov 10, 1838 - Jan 16, 1918

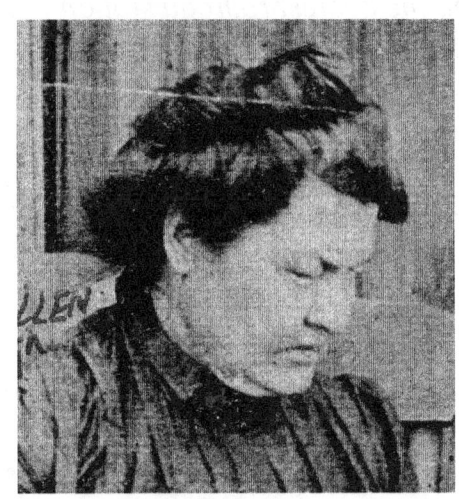

Mary Ellen Bell Goodenough
Aug 28, 1844 - Jun 18, 1921

Children

Mary Ellen	1862 – 1934
George Ferdinand	1864 – 1935
*Isabell (Belle)	1865 – 1896
William	1868 – 1947
Jack, John	1870 – 1920
Constance (Kate)	1874 – 1938
Jane, Delores, Dora (Doll)	1877 – 1966
Samuel A.	1882 – 1927
Benjamin Franklin	1884 – 1941
Clarence Andrew	1886 – 1954

The story goes that when the Goodenough ancestors came to America, they couldn't make the immigration man understand the spelling of their name. Finally, he said, "that's good enough." It was entered on the form as "Goodenough" and the ancestor kept that name. We don't know what the last name was originally. Goodenough is a common surname so I don't know if I believe this story. Another contact had a similar story.

Andrew's parents, Erastus and Marie C., died when he was a child. We have no information on them, but know that Andrew came West with his father's brother, Sam

Goodenough. In the 1860 census, they are in Genoa, Nevada. Sam 46 is tending bar, and Andrew 23 is a teamster. This is also the year Andrew marries Mary Ellen Bell.

Andrew Goodenough was the first man to drive a fourteen-mule team down the Portneuf canyon in the freighting days of 1878 and 1879. He freighted from Corinne, Utah, then the nearest railroad station to Butte, hauling salt for 3 ½ to 4 cents a pound. He went north with salt and south with Bullion Bars. He told of frequent troubles with Indians but has never been scalped. Idaho in Retrospect Idaho State Journal Pocatello Idaho April 13 1958.

My husband Jack and I visited a historic bar in Nevada that could have been where Sam served drinks. The Genoa Bar was used in many western films. It became tradition for women to throw their bras to the rafters. One time Raquel Welch was filming in the area. She was asked if she would like to add her bra to the collection. She said only if they removed all the other bras! They did as she asked. Now all the other bras are in an open door safe to be viewed by the patrons.

In 1872, charges were brought against Andrew Goodenough and Sam Bell (his father-in-law) for diverting someone else's water right from a creek. They were fined $500. Both were excommunicated from the LDS church for unchristian-like behavior the next year. Whether the two incidents were related I don't know.

After the move to Idaho, Andrew again makes the legal rolls when he and his son William are charged with stealing and branding a horse in Pocatello, no date.

The 1880 census is where our own James Reid (Gam) becomes entwined with the Goodenoughs. After making his way from Scotland, James's family is in Rhode Island in 1870 and he is still using the surname Miller. In the following 1880 census, James has taken his mother's maiden name of Reid. He is in Oneida, Idaho, age 29, living with the Goodenoughs as a laborer and would marry their 15-yr-old daughter Belle the next year. I have no information of the 10 years between 1870 and 1880, nor why James came West in the first place.

In the 1900 census the Goodenoughs are in the McCammon area where they live until death.

The following was taken from a McCammon history book: *John Andrew Goodenough was born in Rochester New York in 1842. Little is known of his personal history as a young man. He was restless and adventuresome, always looking for new places.*

He met and married Mary Ellen Bell in Nauvoo, Illinois, where she was born in August 1843. John engaged in the freighting business and the young couple moved to Carson City, Nevada, five children were born to them in Carson City.

Then they loaded all their belongings into a covered wagon and moved to Winnemucca Nev. and the freighting business was continued.

Another move brought them safely across the Nevada desert to Corinne Utah. In spite of many Indian raids and massacres occurring at the time, the Goodenoughs came through safely. John Andrew had a great knowledge of Indian habits with his long experience on the freight lines.

Soon restlessness came again and the family moved on to what is now known as Arimo, but at the time (1880 it was Oneida). Andrew Goodenough is credited with driving the first fourteen mule team down the Portneuf canyon back in the freighting days. Here John Andrew ran his freight line from Oneida to Old Fort Hall. The railroads were beginning to come through but the freight business was still booming and the route went on to Arco.

Then the family moved to a place called Marsh Creek, between Oneida and McCammon. Here the family homesteaded a farm and built a large log house on the banks of the creek. There were fish and wild geese and ducks, good farming land and plenty of water and game in the nearby hills. Goodenough Canyon was named for the family and Bell Marsh was named for the mother Mary Bell Goodenough.

Mary Ellen Goodenough was a nurse and midwife. She delivered many babies in the area. She and Dr. Kackley from Soda Springs were friends and together they ministered to the sick during the flu epidemic. A country school was built nearby and boys and girls in the area attended the school.

Andrew and Mary spent their remaining years in this area. Andrew passed away in 1918 and Mary in 1921. They are buried in unmarked graves in the Harkness Cemetery, McCammon, Idaho.

Children of Andrew and Mary Ellen Bell Goodenough

Mary Ellen
June 22, 1862 - Dec 23, 1934
Mary Ellen married Mathew (Jim) Boyle. This is the Boyle family that had the Ferry Ranch in Jackson Hole, Wyoming, where Kittie Reid Blair worked. (Mimi wrote) *Another member of the family I dearly loved was Mary Boyle O'Kelly. She hasn't a lot of musical education but she can play anything you want by ear.*

George Ferdinand
Feb 14, 1864 - Jun 23, 1935
Married Bertha Elizabeth Glodde

Isabell (Belle)
Dec 24, 1865 - Feb 10, 1896
Married James Reid

William
June 22, 1868 - Jan 23, 1947

William married Anna Mae Hargraves Hunter. He was an apt student and learned to play the violin and pump organ. William rode for the Pony Express. He loved the cowboy life, was an especially talented roper and horseman and worked for Harkness Cattle Company. He was skilled with a handgun and rifle and was given the nickname of "Eagle Eye Willie."

When he was 32 he met and married Anna Mae Hargraves Hunter, a petite 17-year-old. He was ready to settle down and became a cattle rancher, farmer, and custom repairman of any wood and iron work. Anna made and sold butter and eggs under the label of "Mary Goodenough's Sweet Cream and Butter."

Jack or John
June 14, 1870 - Sept 21, 1920
Didn't marry

A funny one my Dad remembers hearing is that Jack (or John) went to Alaska in the gold rush days. He was a bachelor always. He was telling the people about how the whales would come up on the beach and suckle their babies. "And those whales, they'd give a thousand gallons of milk!" "You mean to say," someone asked, "that the baby whale would drink a thousand gallons of milk?" Jack answered, "Christ yes, and bunt for more!"

Constance (Kate)
July 6, 1874 - April 20, 1938

Kate married Mayford Lockyear. Kate and Mayford's son, Dick Lockyear, had a limp from Clubfoot, but was able to dance. Clubfoot ran in the Goodenough line. Also Jim Reid's son Jack had the affliction.

Jane, Delores, Dora, (Doll)
Dec 19, 1877 - April 30, 1966
Married Jake Baird

Robert Reid was staying with Doll and Jake Baird while he worked for Nels Just on the hydroelectric dam project on the Blackfoot River. Agnes Just stayed with the Bairds too while she taught school at Cedar Creek. When Agnes and Robert were married, they chose the Baird home, by then in Springfield, Idaho, for the wedding.

Doll was in a rest home at the end. Mimi received a letter from her every few months but she stopped writing. Agnes wanted to visit her, but they said she wouldn't know her.

Samuel A
Nov 29, 1882 - May 11, 1927
Married Cora Idella (Ida) Johnson

Benjamin Franklin
Jan 17, 1884 - Sep 18, 1941
Married Alta Lightner

Clarence Andrew
Dec 14, 1886 - Dec 5, 1954
Married Clara Elvira Frosig

This remarkable photo was taken west of McCammon on the old Goodenough Ranch in 1896. It shows three generations - Bell, Goodenough and Reid, and was taken not long after Isabell died. Kittie wrote the names of the people in the photo: *George Goodenough, wife Mary and children to the left, Jack Goodenough* (above the Reids), *Jim, Robert* (tallest child), *Don, William, Richard, Kittie, and James Reid, Great Grandfather Samuel Bell, Grandmother Mary Goodenough, Grandfather Andrew Goodenough, Will Goodenough far back on the wagon.*

I wonder if the photo showed other people before it was torn. Children Kate and Dora were married and gone, but Ben, Sam and Clarence were young enough to be home and are missing from the photo. This is the only picture I have that is known to be Sam Bell. We can imagine that James Reid was with Belle's parents trying to figure out what to do with his six kids after the death of their mother.

(Mimi wrote) *Fred Bennett always said, "The women of the Goodenough family were the best damn women in the world."... My husband's mother was Belle and she married Jim Reid at Albion in the early seventies. My husband has been gone twenty years and we never kept in touch with his Goodenough relatives but all I knew were fine people.*

Mary Ellen has several pictures and in most she is turning her head. I asked a contact from ancestry.com if she had some problem with her eye because one picture looked like it could be. This contact confirmed it.

Mary Ellen came to the Just house to stay overnight on her way to the hills to see her daughters Kate and Doll. Emma tells of her visit in her diaries. She slept with Emma as guests were apt to do. I bet she loved seeing Robert and her great-grand boys.

Another time word was sent that Mary Ellen had died and Robert went to inform Kate and Doll of it.

Robert's Parents

James (Gam) and Isabell Goodenough Reid

James (Gam) Reid
March 4, 1850 - Jan 11, 1936

Isabell Goodenough Reid
Dec 24, 1865 - Feb 10, 1896

Children

James Edward (Jim)	1882 - 1927
***Robert Ezekiel**	**1884 - 1947**
Donald Duncan (Don)	1886 - 1960
Nellie	1887 - 1890
William Charles (Bill)	1891 - 1967
Richard Thomas (Dick)	1892 - 1959
Katie Ellen (Kittie)	1894 - 1993

Scotland birth records have a birthdate for James Miller of March 4, 1849, but all other records show the year as 1850. There is a census in Westray, Scotland, in 1851 where he is 1 year old with his parents and sister. In 1861 he is 11 and there are 4 more siblings.

We know he was born in Scotland, which is verified in the censuses of 1851, 1861 and 1870. Interestingly in all the following censuses it says he was born in Rhode Island, and all the children claim that their father was born in Rhode Island. I think maybe he claimed this so he could homestead land in America. Another discrepancy is the Idaho Death Index has his birthdate as March 15, 1855. I have no idea how that happened or why. The "find a grave" site has his birth date correct.

There is a family story that James worked on a whaling vessel in Scotland. He also was said to have sailed around the tip of South America. He was in Rhode Island in 1870, twenty years old, and by the 1875 Rhode Island census he is gone. I guess it is possible he could have sailed from Rhode Island and came to Idaho from the west coast. One of those things we will probably never know.

James married Isabelle when she was 15 and he was 30. They had 7 children in the 15 years they were married before Isabelle died. Dad thought she had heart problems. Her beautiful metal headstone is in the Robin Cemetery off the Arimo exit. It is many miles after the exit and by a farm house. The headstone reads: *Belle Reid died Feb 10, 1896 age 30 years 1 month and 15 days. In After time, we'll meet.*

Robin Cemetery

(Mimi wrote) *The most heart-breaking story Father Reid ever told me was that after his wife died, he was left with six children and several hundred dollars in doctor bills. He was working for twenty dollars a month, but he paid off the staggering sum. That's where my boys got thrift and integrity.*

James Reid and friend Ed Murphy

The only other picture of Isabell, with Dick

Jim, Robert, Don, Dick, Bill, Kittie and James (Gam)

This cropped section of the bigger picture shown earlier shows the six motherless Reid children with their Dad.

All three older Reid boys, Jim, Robert and Don left after their mother's death and didn't live with the family thereafter. Jim started his lifetime career as a sheep herder.

Don lived with a family in McCammon, the Howells. When Ginger Reid was teaching school in McCammon many years later, she stayed in the same house that Don lived in after his mother died.

Robert was 12 or 13 and worked for a dry farmer in Downey, the Dixons. Many years later, our grandma Mimi and Grandy were in Pocatello and ran into the Dixons. The woman exclaimed, "Oh, Zekie! You're so handsome!"

(Mimi wrote) *The Dixons took Bob (Zeke) in when his mother died and I loved them for their kindness to him. I just met Mrs. Dixon once.*

Mom (Alma) met a relative of this family when she was on her *Along the Rivers* book selling tour in the same area. This woman was happy to buy 5 books.

Following Belle's death, James put the three youngest kids in an orphanage in Salt Lake. That didn't last long. When it was learned the children had head lice they were brought home to live with family. (I think with the Andrew Goodenough grandparents)

Dick 9, Kittie 5 and Bill 7

James Edward Miller wrote a letter on January 20, 1887 or 89 (illegible) from Mount Pleasant, Pierowall, Westray, Orkney, Scotland, to James (Gam) and Belle after they had two children.

Our dear son, daughter and children. We hope that you are all well. We are longing much for a letter from you. I wrote you last summer and we have been expecting word from you ever since. I hope you will answer this right away and let me know how you are getting along and how our daughter Bella is and how our little boys is and if they are growing big fellows and if they are learning the Catechism and if Jamie is able to hold the (?) yet or is he going to school you did not tell us the name of the other young man yet (Robert) we hope he is well and growing a big fellow too he will soon be helping his mother. Dear son and daughter I fear you are a great distance from any church or Sabbath School you will need Salvation through a Crucified Redeemer as there is a great responsibility upon your God give them to you teaching them and raising and bringing them up in the nature and administered of the Lord that when we have to stand before the Great White throne to give in our account that we be not charged with neglect or have remorse of continence . . . to be very careful and punctual in teaching the children the way of . . .

James owned land called "Horse Island" in the big Snake River that could only be reached by ferry. Gwen remembers going to a picnic/fishing party for her church when she was a little girl on Horse Island. She recalled an old man helping her brother Don bait his hook. She knows this must have been James. In the early 20's a huge dam was built at American Falls which backed up the river and completely covered Horse Island with water. Gam received a sum of money for the loss of his land.

Most of the pictures of Gam later in life were with the grandkids.

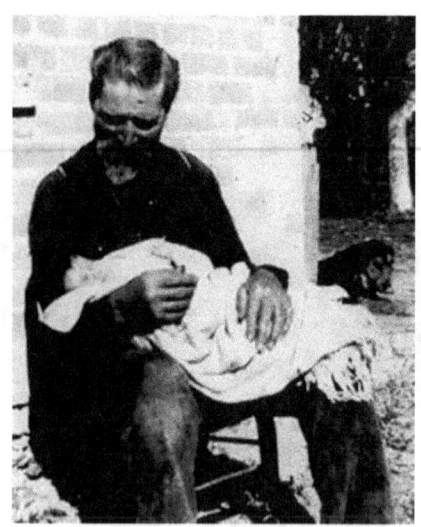

Gam with Doug

Gam, Eldro and Fred

I asked Dad what kind of a man his grandfather was. He said, "*He was a good, kind guy, he wasn't tall like Dad but more medium build*".

I don't know if Gam spoke Spanish, or where he would have learned it, but he used it some.

(Part of a letter that must have been to Nellie, I wonder if he is talking about Belle) *She had been operated on for appendicitis I guess it run her strength down low. The Just Reids and myself are all well, Thanks to the powers that be. Bueno Dias*

Mina niece
Jas Reid

Letters from Gam

Aberdeen Ida 12/20/10
(After Eldro was born)
Dear children,

I read your letter was very glad to hear from you glad to hear you are all well again. I suppose the little fellow is great company for all of you they are generally as a rule. I am very glad to hear that he is good a baby, his dad was the best baby I ever saw. You couldn't tell he was in the house, so if he takes after him, you won't have much trouble with him. But those Daddy Reid hands and feet I guess are all right for a big boy but when he grows up to match those hands you will be quite proud of him. I am very much obliged to you for your invitation to come and eat Christmas dinner with him but it is out of the question. I can't come as I am looking after the Tarbet place at present. The young man that has charge of it has gone home to spend the holidays and to get himself a wife and that kind of thing must not be put off, if it can be helped. I will come up some day and see him if possible and I think it will be.

James Reid

Shelley Idaho Dec 18, 1923
Dear Kit,

I got out of the hospital but, am not well yet and it looks as though I never will be. But I may get all right after a while. I have had some bad luck here since I got out. The Standard Bank has gone out of business and I lost all the money I had, about $600, more than I could stand to lose. My doctor and hospital bills was about that amount. Well, what are you doing there? can't be much to do up there in the winter time. Agnes says she wrote you to come down here. But you haven't shown up yet or said anything about it. I have very little reason to write and what I have don't amount to anything. Been fine weather here so far. Write and let me know how you are and little Buck is getting along and what your prospects are and everything. Wishing you a merry Xmas and happy new year. I am your father

P S We are all well here. Eldro got his arm broken a while ago but is getting along alright. I can't write since my troubles, hand wiggles.   Well good by J R

Shelley Idaho Jan 6, 1924
My Dear Kit

I received your letter a few days ago. Was very glad to hear from you, am glad that you and little Buck are well, that you have a pretty good job and that Buck can go to school. I suppose you have quite a little snow up there by this time. We haven't much here yet but, may get plenty before long, it has been quite cold here. Too cold for me, as I haven't hardly been out of the house all winter and when I do go out, I nearly chill to death.

I don't seem to get much better for some reason or other, can't get any strength. My wound is nearly healed up but, it is quite sore and my legs is so stiff that I can't hardly walk. I may have to see the doctor again with it.

I told you that I lost all my money when the Standard bank broke but I didn't (lose) quite as much as I thought I had. I gave the doctor and the hospital over $400 and they got their checks in just in time so I am that much ahead. Dick and Bill lost $150 also I lost nearly $300 so you see I am broke but maybe we will be able to stand it. The folks here are all well. Mabel Bennett has been sick for the last few days with a sore throat but is better now. Well there is no news here to tell you so I will bid you good by with all kinds of good wishes.

Your father Jas Reid
PS I am pretty badly disgusted with myself, I'll tell you, dad.

Firth Idaho June 13, 1924
(to granddaughter Nellie, Jim Reid's daughter)
My Dear Nellie,

I received your letter a few days ago and you bet I was glad to hear from you. Very glad to hear you are doing well. There is no news here, I was in Firth, 11th, saw your mother and the little ones and your cousins, the Misses Murphy. They are looking fine as mother, everybody here also feeling well. We are having better weather here now and things are looking better, grass and grain growing, beets and spuds and your aunty Kit and her boy is going up to Jackson Hole again this summer, will go soon. I, myself am going up to the mountains right away, it's too lonesome down here, for me. Wish you could come and stay with me, then we would be as happy and cozy as a pair of turtle doves, or some other pets. Well, I must bid you goodbye wishing ever so much good luck and ever so many good times and hoping you will enjoy them and accept a kiss
James Reid write soon

My Dear Nellie My Bonnie Wee Lassie

I got your letter 3 or 4 days ago, was very glad to hear from you. I was beginning to think you had thrown off on me and I had lost my only sweet heart.

There is no news here worth mentioning, only we have a new baby boy here at the Reid Just ranch. A big fine fellow with black hair and dark blue eyes named Wallace at my suggestion. You know they have one named Douglass and I said if you are naming your sons after Scottish heroes call him Wallace which they did. And if he makes as brave and loyal a man as the man he is named after he will be all right. But of course, the name is of no moment so we must take chances.

You say you are very homesick it's too bad, I wish I was a thousand times a millionaire and see that you had all the fun and good times you could wish. I'd take you all over the world and if we didn't have a good time, it would be because we didn't know how to enjoy life. But such things have denied us for the lack the wherewith but even wealth doesn't make happiness so we must make the best of our condition and be good to each other and be friendly with our friends and our neighbors. Now you may think I am trying to preach to you but I'm too hardened an old sinner for that.

I was in Firth a short time ago and saw your folks they were all well and looking well satisfied with things in general. Your father was still up to Arco and they didn't know when he would be down. I must make another trip to the mountains this summer and am in hopes it will be the last. Now I am going to close and not bother you more with my silly talk. Good bye and good luck attend you is my sincere wish of your old granddad. Write again and tell me all about yourself.

James Reid

James was known to love the ocean surely because he grew up next to it on the Orkney Islands. He was 17 when he came to America. Jerrie Reid, Eldro's wife, painted a picture of the ship "Old Ironsides" for Gam.

(Jerrie's letter to Mimi after Gam got her gift of the painting)

Dear Mrs. Reid I'm so glad Gam thought the picture was "purty good". I really do know that that is much from him. But if I had nothing more than the pleasure of being at your place, while I painted it, I should be more than repaid. A good word from him makes it even better.

He didn't have a frame big enough to put it in, so cut off the whitecaps in the foreground. Mimi wrote to Jerrie about it and this was her response:

(Jerrie wrote) *How relieved I was when I found what the "tragedy" was! I was so worried and frightened for the moment, that is not really a tragedy at all. Yes, he is a realist the "realist of the realists," but he takes little Dougie for walks and helps him pick flowers for his mama, so what matter if he doesn't understand that an oil painting must have certain proportions to be right. He will still enjoy it and after all, it was made for him.*

(Fred, my dad, wrote this postcard to Gam, May 23 of 1928 in childish longhand)
Dear Gam will you kindly water my garden?
Fred

(Jerrie wrote) *Gam stopped here yesterday as you know, he was so nice. He and I talked and talked and he was so gracious about the little dinner I fixed him.*

Gam would say when someone asked how he was: "*I feel like Hell and a damn sight worse!*" Dad would answer after the same question: "*poor to middl'n.*"

James Reid was a great rawhide braider, like Fred Bennett. The two men had plans to spend the winter together at Fred Bennett's home, braiding rawhide, but that was the year Fred Bennett died.

Fred and Alma's garden was in the same place James had the family garden. Doug said it was good sized. Fred said he wouldn't let you eat corn until it was too old.

Fred remembers Gam helping Doug play records on the phonograph. He must have broken one and Gam said, "*that's ok Douglass.*"

Gam carved Dad a toy boat. It was neat with a weighted bottom so it would stay floating upright. Wally had one too, so maybe all the kids were given one. There is a picture of one.

James Reid proved up on a homestead in Brockman, Idaho, and had a homestead on Homer Creek. Dick and Bill also homesteaded there.

James gave Kittie an old family bible that is believed to be his or his father's. We found it after Uncle Doug died and it can be viewed in the old house.

In later years Gam came to live in the old homestead cabin north and east of Agnes and Robert's home. He lived there about 13 years, coming down for meals and to work in his garden that he had at the bottom of the hill. He spent winters there and much of the summer in the Blackfoot hills. The grandkids had a very close relationship with their grandfather.

(Mimi wrote) *Gam has a new hat. An $8 Stetson. He said "Well, this hat might last me as long as I'll need a hat." I said "Gam, Gam, Scotchman would not die and leave a good hat like that, half worn out." He laughed so I guess he has decided to winter.*

(Mimi wrote after Gam was sick and living mostly at Dick and Milly's) *Gam Reid stayed just one week and the day he was going I wanted to get a good picture of him. Just as he was ready to go, I discovered I had left my Kodak at the Larsen's the day before. So, I rushed down ahead of him and met him there by Jim's. After I had taken the pictures, he said "Well, this may be the last picture you'll get of your old dad." Then he tied his lines and came over and kissed me and told me how he had always loved me. I was like Dougie. He says, "I cry and I bellar" and I almost did.*

(Mimi wrote) *Father Reid died. He had been with the brother at Springfield (Dick) for three months or so but at Christmas time he came back and stayed a week. The* *weather was cold and he was very miserable so we moved out of our room and gave it to him. Christmas tree and all. A few days after Christmas he decided he felt better down at Dick's so Rufus took him back. Then a little while later they brought him up to us for he had decided to go to the hospital. We took him to the hospital January 3 and he died there a week later. We buried him at American Falls very near the spot where I first met him twenty-nine years ago (1907). It was too bad he could not have gone sooner for he was sort of irresponsible. He drew out a thousand dollars cash from his life's savings and bought Dick's wife a Dodge car, then he bought her a Maytag and other things too numerous to mention, while his own girl washes on a board. The insurance was made to Kit so she got that, a thousand, and there was enough in the bank to give $325.00 to each of the children. Not very good pay for sharing your home with anyone for twelve years but I was lucky, at that, for he was always quite pleasant to be around and was lovely to the children.*

James Reid died before Gwen came to the family. Doug was 9 years old and remembered him well.

Isn't this a cool shot of the Reids?

Father James (Gam) Robert, Bill, Dick and Kittie

It was a tradition to get a picture of all the brothers with their Mom at any big Reid summer party. This one shows that Bill and Kit were at this one too.

Children of James and Isabell Goodenough Reid

James (Jim) Edward Reid
Aug 7, 1882 - Nov 25, 1947
Jim married Lymeda Murphy, they later divorced.

Jim and Don looked the most alike but they parted their hair on opposite sides. Jim was a loner, herded sheep and was seldom with his wife and children. Mom remembers seeing him once in his sheep camp. For a time he lived in a camp in Kit's yard.

Jim and Lymeda were not involved much with Grandy's family. Dad said they rarely saw them growing up, even though they lived in Firth. (Vin said) *"Mimi didn't like his wife and Jim didn't like her much either."* Emma talks quite often about Lymeda in her diaries and seemed to like her.

Lymeda and Jim divorced at some point. Kate, Belle's sister, had died and left Mayford Lockyear a widow, and then Lymeda and Mayford were married.

Children of James and Lymeda Reid

Nellie Isabell
April 27, 1907 - July 10, 1993

When my Mom and Dad were stationed in Georgia, Dad wrote: *We got a letter from Nellie today. She wants us to go see her if we can. It's about 120 miles up there, I think.*

They didn't see her then, but when they were semi-retired from ranch work, they, along with Vin and Gwen, went back East to visit my sister Donna and saw Nellie who lived in College Park, Maryland, with her husband John and kids, John Jr. and Margaret Ann Daley, and worked for the FBI. Dad said she was kind of a problem girl growing up but she was a wonderful adult. She had dropped the "Nellie" name and was going by "Marguerite."

Nellie was interested in history and kept in touch with her Dad's cousin Bessie. Nellie, in turn, corresponded with Gwen Reid. It is through this connection that we have the photos of James Edward Miller's children and his priceless correspondence.

This unsigned letter was found in the old house. Kathy Mattson Christenson took it in to be scanned at the Bingham County Historical Society. The description of Emma, our ancestor, was so sweet and complete that we knew we needed to give the author credit. The search was on to solve the mystery. With a bit of connecting the dots we decided it was Nellie Reid.

(Nellie wrote) *We had cousins down the road 12 miles, my Uncle Bob Reid's children, and they had relatives in England. They would give us the old magazines and lend us the books just as a lending library. We had lots of time for reading.*

Grandma (Emma) Just – we didn't have any grandmothers, both grandmothers had died when our parents were small so these cousins Uncle Bob's children had the most wonderful grandma. And she was the only grandma that we knew too, she was a tiny little woman from England. She was so small that she wore skirts and shirt waist blouses. She had a little bustle that she tied around her waist under her skirt and that held the skirt on as she didn't have the hips, she was so small. She always rode side saddle. On her 61 birthday she rode sidesaddle 12 miles up in the hills and spent the day with my mother. She brought her oldest grandsons with her. One was 12 and the other 10. They came on their ponies and she came on her old mare. When she was 65 her family thought that she should have a buggy and they had to teach the old mare to pull a buggy because she was used to being ridden. Grandma Just had to change to a buggy and she felt very bad about giving up her horse and teaching it new tricks.

James Everett
Nov 6, 1908 - Sept 3, 1987

Harold Edward
March 25, 1912 - Oct 23, 1951

Donald Lloyd
Nov 18, 1918 - Dec 22, 1985

Margaret M
Dec 6, 1918 - Feb 9, 1985

Jack Neal
Feb 12, 1923 - July 21, 1990

End of Jim and Lymeda's children

Robert (Grandy, Zeke, Rufus, Bob, R. E.) **Reid**
March 10, 1884 – Sept 20, 1947
Married Agnes Katherine Just

Don Duncan Reid
Jan 29, 1886 - Nov 14, 1960
Married Hilma Olson Wring

Children of Don and Hilma

Donald
Aug 1907 - Jan 1908

Ruth Iantha
(adopted)
Nov 20, 1912 – July 30, 1994
Ruth married Clarence Verbeck, children, Reid and Grant. They came once in a while to stay with the Reids.

Don and Hilma had a very happy marriage. Hilma died young. When Gwen came to the valley to interview for the teaching job, two of the school board members were at Hilma's funeral - Robert as a brother-in-law and the Wring man as the father. Alvin Just (later Gwen said it was Frank Pratt) did the interviewing.

(Grandy wrote in Portland where he was living with Don and taking asthma treatments) *Don is just about as wheezy as I am. I can't hardly tell which of us is me sometimes. But I just wait around a while and if anyone goes to work, why that's Don, so that's how we tell. Another way we tell is by the one that catches hell, that's Don again.*

Don worked as a mechanic at a shipyard. They moved to California for a few miserable years then he returned to Idaho staying with Kit or Mimi. He died in California.

Hilma, Don, Bill, Robert, and Bert Wring (Hilma's brother)

After Hilma died, Don married Dell Rovetta. She had two kids from a previous marriage, Tasha and Peter.

End of Don and Hilma's children

Nellie Reid
Oct 19, 1887 – Aug 1890. Nellie only lived three years and we do not have photos of her.

Richard Thomas (Dick) Reid
Jan 29, 1884 - Nov 14, 1960
Married Millie Parsons

Millie, Dick, Norma

Millie in her later years

Dick lived in Springfield. Dad remembers going to see Dick in Arizona where he lived in a sanitarium, probably with TB. He had diabetes, asthma problems, and he stuttered.

(Gwen wrote) *Dick was very charming and handsome like his brothers. Something that struck me was how much the 4 boys, Grandy, Don, Bill and Dick were alike in manners and gestures though they never lived together as a family. It was almost uncanny.*

Dick and Bill lived in the Springfield area and were friends with Bus Driscoll, Jack Clark's grandpa. Bus told this story about his friend Dick Reid that stuttered. Someone asked directions somewhere and Dick tried several times to get it out. Finally, he said in frustration, *"by the time I tell you, you could have been there!"*

Both Dick and Bill Reid served in France in World War I. My Dad thinks Dick worked with the horses, pulling supplies or equipment. Robert was married and had 2 kids when the war was on so wasn't called to serve.

Bill and Dick homesteaded in Long Valley, Idaho.

Daughter of Dick and Millie

Norma
Nov 13, 1928 – Dec 1, 2012

(Mimi wrote) *Norma was my husband's favorite niece.* Norma married Don Shelman and had children, divorced and later married Delayne Driscoll (Jack Clark's uncle) and divorced. She was a beautiful, sweet woman.

(Gwen wrote) *Millie was a good wife and mother. Theirs was a true love marriage. Millie was almost a chain smoker and ended up with terrible emphysema and oxygen 24 hours a day. She lived 14 years longer than Dick but suffered terribly.*

When Millie died (1973) her son-in-law, Gene Shelman (then separated from Norma), came to Blackfoot area to see where he could help. He was killed in an automobile accident on his way back to Springfield, so Millie and Gene were buried 1 day apart - tough for the Grandchildren Ann, Kay, Richard Jr. and Pamela.

End of Dick and Millie's family

William Charles (Bill) **Reid**
July 18, 1891 - Nov 18, 1967
Married Mae Martin

(Mimi wrote) *married once and regretted it.*

Bill was a bachelor for many years then married. It didn't last long; they stayed married but didn't live together. Bill lived next to Dick in a sheep camp. Dad said that Millie liked Bill and it wasn't a problem. Bill was found dead, probably of a heart attack, at his table.

(Mimi wrote to Millie after his death) *I was sorry for you that after all the years you watched over Bill it had to be that way, but don't blame yourself. Just be glad that he suffered so little at the end. He had suffered enough through the years with every breath he drew.*

(Gwen wrote) *Many years later I received a call from First Security Bank, Blackfoot, asking if we knew a William Charles Reid. Upon investigation, we found his savings account had never been claimed. It amounted to about $500 and through our efforts and Reid Larsen, attorney, Aunt Kit got this inheritance and had her teeth fixed.*

Katie Ellen (Kittie) **Reid**
Jan 10, 1894 - Oct 23, 1993

Kittie married Roy Bower and they had one child, Roy Noel Jr. (Buck) and later divorced. She later married Ed Blair and they had one child, Kathleen.

Kittie was only 2 when her mother died. She went to the orphanage with her older brothers Will and Dick for a time until they were brought back to live with their grandparents, the Goodenoughs until she was 11. Then she went to live with her dad in American Falls.

James Reid worked for the railroad in American Falls. (Gwen wrote) *Kittie about 12 years old had to walk the railroad tracks to get to school and her father had warned her not to talk to any strangers along the way. One day two or three men were by the railroad when Kittie came along. One of the men asked, "What's your name young lady?" She answered, "What's it to you?" The man threw back his head and laughed and laughed and finally said, "Well, I think your brother Bob just married my daughter Agnes." Such was Kittie's introduction to Nels. Kittie felt terrible to think she had been rude and thought he would never forgive her. But soon afterwards the Justs invited Kittie to come visit them and meet Bob Reid's wife, Agnes, who lived with Nels and Emma. Nels made a point to meet Kittie's train in Firth and bring her in the horse drawn wagon to their home. After that they were very good friends.*

(Agnes wrote on her way to Boise) *I dropped a letter along the tracks that Kit will get on her way from school tonight.* Mimi must have <u>literally</u> dropped the letter along the tracks.

Kittie rode horses a lot when a young girl.

(American Falls from Robert to Agnes) *Hilma and I have been alone and had a good talk about things. The kids have grown a great deal since I saw them last. Kit is quite a big girl now. She has been combing my hair.*

(Mimi wrote) *I cannot remember just how we contacted B.M. Bower but perhaps it was through her publisher. My sister-in-law (Kit) was with us at the time and Bower took her back to California to "baby sit." She had a little girl, Delta Frances. She also had a young son.* (So young that he had to have his mother's permission to marry Kit).

Dad told of when Kittie was living with her mother-in-law, that Charlie Russell came to visit and she met the famous artist. They lived in California for a couple of years, and son Roy (Buck) was born. Dad thinks the marriage lasted about 6 years. Kit was divorced and then she and Buck came back to Idaho. Buck didn't have much contact with his dad, and Kit didn't get financial support for him. Dad remembers seeing Roy (senior) when he came to visit when Buck was about 10 or 12. Kit kept in touch with B. M. Bower for many years.

Kittie worked at a candy company in Jackson Hole. The recipe for caramels that Mom and Gwen used for their candy came from her and that job. Debbie Reid-Oleson keeps the caramel tradition alive.

Son of Kittie and Roy Bower

Roy Noel Bower Jr.
"Buck" to the Reids
Apr 25, 1915 - May 22, 1983

This is a portion of a letter by Buck's daughter Joan Bower Hosey: *Roy Bower Sr. died in 1936 at Depot Bay, Oregon. He was killed trying to rescue a man and his son and a neighbor boy who couldn't make it back into the harbor safely as they were having engine trouble in a storm. Jack Chambers, his friend and helper on this boat the "Cara Lou," was killed also. There is a monument erected on the sea wall by the Oregonian newspaper at Depot Bay in memory of Roy and Jack. Every year on Memorial Day the people and fishermen at Depot Bay celebrate the Fleet of Flowers. This was originally started for Roy and Jack. Over the years they have enlarged it to include anyone lost at sea.*

Buck married Helen Marti in 1938, and very soon Kittie was a grandmother to twin girls, Joan and Jean, a grandson Ronald, then Karlee, another girl. The family came to Firth to be close to Kit when Buck was in the army but lived in Oregon after.

Later Buck and his family lived in Weiser. He worked at a cement plant and lost an arm in a work accident. Roy had cancer and died in 1983.

Buck and Helen Bower

Helen made wonderful stuffed dolls. I remember getting one with a satin green dress and red yarn hair. It was a double doll that if you flipped the skirt over, it had a black yarn haired doll with a calico blue dress on the other end. It was lost in our house fire.

(Mimi wrote) in a letter to Buck) *You started out without very good health and had two stepfathers so I think you have traveled a long way in the right direction. You've always remembered that you had a family and have done your best to give them everything they wanted.*

When Fred Bennett's wife Agnes died, and Kit was divorced, she went to help his family out. Fred was in his 50's and Kit much younger but the family hoped they would fall for each other. Dad thinks Fred had feelings for Kit but she wasn't interested.

Kit married George Lawton. This marriage didn't last long and they had no children. It was February, "the winter that never snowed" 1929/1930, they had a picnic in the grove when Kit, George and Buck were there visiting. There is a picture of Buck 15, Vin 14 and dad 10 most visible. Buck and Vin are holding airplanes they made. Robert and Mimi, and George Lawton are sitting.

(Mimi wrote) *Grace Williams got Kittie her telephone. They wanted her to have one for years but Grace made it happen.*

One time George bought a team of mules and a white top buggy. Dad remembers they used the mules on the buck rake. They lived in the red house for a while one summer. Kit's marriage to Lawton lasted 2 or 3 years but he was worthless.

Kit worked at the Ferry Ranch at Jackson Hole, Wyoming, sometime after she divorced Lawton. She met Ed Blair there, and they were married in 1929. Their marriage lasted about 30 years until his death. It wasn't a wonderful marriage either. He smoked and cussed and was sometimes crude. They moved from Jackson and lived in the red house with their daughter Kathleen.

Daughter of Kittie and Ed Blair

Kathleen Belle Blair
Jan 26, 1931 - July 14, 1948

Kathleen sang at Grandy's funeral.

She had graduated from high school, and had been looking for a job in Idaho Falls. She stepped off the Greyhound bus, walked behind it, and was hit and killed by a truck. The accident happened close to the river bridge in Firth.

(Gwen wrote) *But each experience – good or tragic has embedded its mark in Kitties' pleasantly lined face. A beautiful lady who has survived the worst and is ready for tomorrow. Kittie and Kathleen were present at our wedding in Aberdeen in 1936. A very special memory for us.*

Kittie and Ed lived by Mimi and Grandy for a time, then bought a house in Firth and settled permanently there. Ed worked wherever he could find a job. (Gwen wrote) *With little money but a lot of work they made the little shanty into a very comfortable home, complete with a large beautiful yard and big garden.*

Ed Blair was telling Dad about a ewe that died. "It was just lay'n there, one leg kind of up like that… and the other leg kinda over like this… it was just lay'n there, dead. Deader than hell!"

Ed Blair drove the school bus on our route, probably right before George Macanelly. Dad remembers Ted telling about how Ed drove (badly).

Ed was in poor health for many years and Kittie took care of him. At the time she was also nursing her brother Don that lived there too. Both died in 1960.   (Mimi wrote) *When Dick died Kittie had Ed, when Ed died, she had Don, when Don died, she had Bill, when Bill died, she had no men folks left.*

Kittie's cooking specialty was salt water taffy; it was perfection. The rest of us try to imitate her method, but no one has yet achieved it. The candy was poured onto a wet dish and would be folded over to trap air in it. When it was cool enough to handle it would be stretched and folded over until it was no longer pliable. Then it was brittle and broke into serving size pieces. Dad remembered Kit walking towards the crew, pulling a rope of her famous taffy, for a work break treat. Kit would come to every Reid party, and usually brought a batch of her delicious taffy.

Kit Blair was known for making head cheese. Whenever anyone would kill a hog, the head was given to Kit; she would then give half of the head cheese back. The head would be boiled; the meat and gelatin were formed into a mold. This would be eaten sliced and cold. The Reids loved it.

(Gwen wrote) *Kittie never demanded much besides life's necessities. She treasured the dish cupboard made by her father James Reid.* (Given to her family in Oregon.)

One time she expressed a desire for a matched set of dishes. She had never had one. So Vin and Gwen bought her a four-place setting and insisted she use them every day. She did.

Once Fred and Alma went to visit Kit on her birthday and asked what they could do to make it special. She answered that they could let her cook them a complete dinner just to prove she could. And she did.

(Gwen wrote) *Kit started sewing for a few of her friends. When others found what a beautiful seamstress she was, they brought sewing to her, until many times she was literally snowed under. I imagine she has done sewing for nearly every family in the Firth area at one time or another. She is truly an artist with every article she makes, and not only is she a perfectionist with her sewing, but with her handwork, knitting and crocheting too.*

(Mimi wrote) *Aunt Kit does beautiful sewing and is well paid for it. She has many friends and no enemies. That is living fully I think.*

(Gwen wrote) *Kit probably didn't go to any schooling after grade 8. Training in any skill was self-taught and very effectively.*

(Gwen wrote) *Kit loved plants and could make anything grow. She talks to them and treats them as if they are her children. Kit was almost poetic in her observations of ordinary things, butterflies, birds, tiny growing things, or a spider web. She finds beauty in everything. She was especially fond of lady bugs and whether by choice or by accident she became a collector of them. She loved her yard and enjoys everything from a tiny cedar tree seedling to her apple tree with 5 varieties.*

(Gwen wrote) *She was very knowledgeable but quite shy, even tempered, used excellent grammar, and hated smoking and drinking. If she had a fault, it was that she wasn't confident.*

(Iris Pratt Just wrote of Kittie Blair in a newspaper in celebration of her 90th birthday) *I suppose I first remember her at the Reid's when she and her son came back to Idaho after her divorce from a son of authoress B. M. Bower. She worked around the neighborhood as was much in demand to take care of the new mothers and babies in the homes..........She was an excellent seamstress and had more sewing than she could do. Her eyesight is very good and even now at 90 years she sees better without her glasses than many people do with theirs.* The only glasses she ever owned were from a rack in the drugstore. In her very advanced years, she used a walker.

Kittie lived in Firth and Iris went over often to check on her. (Iris wrote) *One day, I planned to go over in the evening but for some reason I decided to go earlier.* She found Kit on the kitchen floor, and asked what she was doing down there and Kittie answered, "I'm just waiting for you." She had broken her hip but after surgery she was soon up and around.

This photo is of Aunt Kit and Mimi. How I wish I could visit them now. After Mimi died, Doug spent many days at Kit's helping her. Later he moved in and took care of her until her death at 99 years of age. He then continued to live at Kit's until he came to Fred's house for the last months of his life.

One year when a friend of the family turned 100 years old, Kittie and Doug peeled and dried enough apples to make 100 little packages and mailed them to Georgia. Kit was in her 90's.

Kittie was a truly wonderful woman with plenty of hardship including losing a daughter. (Gwen wrote) *For the most part Aunt Kittie found great pleasure loving all her brother Bob's grandchildren and oh, how she was loved by everyone.*

Robert E. Reid and Agnes Just Reid

Robert Ezekiel Reid
March 10, 1884 - Sept 20, 1947

Agnes Katherine Just Reid
Sept 7, 1886 - Aug 7, 1976

Children

Eldro	1910 - 1993
Robert Vincent (Vin)	1914 – 2009
Fred	1919 – 2013
Douglass	1926 – 2012
Wallace	1929 – 2015

Bob lived with his mother's sister, Doll Baird, and her husband, Jake, when he had a job working for Nels Just building a hydroelectric dam on the Blackfoot River above the home place. Our grandma, Agnes Just, was home from college at Albion when she and her father, Nels, rode up in a buggy to look at the progress. This was the first time she saw him.

(Mimi wrote) *There was a little school open here at Cedar Creek, my future husband was one of the seven students going to the school. I first met him when he was working with my brothers on a power project for my dad, up the river. I know very well today how he looked, best looking person in a Mackinaw coat I have ever seen."*

When Mimi finished her schooling, she took a job teaching at the Cedar Creek school, boarding with the Bairds as well.

Bob, who hadn't had much formal schooling, was Mimi's student. The school sat up the hollow north from where the Alridge School would later be. Mimi said of their teacher/student relationship, *"I only taught him to love me."*

(Mimi wrote) *Yes, I taught school for two whole months. Just long enough to get the interest of my oldest student, a year later we were married. I had gone to Normal School with the bold statement that I did not expect to teach, but I did expect to be a mother and I thought that might be good preparation.*

We still have a box of letters back and forth between our grandparents before and after they were married. Agnes was always Agnes, Robert was Rufus, Zeke or R. E. There were several that had the name on the envelope, for example *"Agnes, Kindness of Frank."* They would catch someone going that way and not use the postal system.

These letters are so sweet and romantic.

My Dear Rufus,
   Got your letter tonight and it made me real happy for the first time today. I did not cry at all though darling, just felt forsaken. I cried out all of my troubles in your dear arms. Tonight you are so happy and you have made others happy too I know. Were you lonely in Pocatello? I have thought of you so much today. I went away up on the hill and waited until after I heard the whistle of the train, I knew it was taking with it all that this world holds most dear to me. Monte was afraid I was sad I know, for he came away up on the hill and looked for me. No, I was not as happy as I looked when you saw me last, but I was full of excitement which made me seem so.

   Monte is so much like Blue in traveling. Charlie and Fritz are here tonight so there are six in the kitchen, have plenty of company but no one to love me. Charlie came in and talked with me awhile. He is my dear little brother seems like he ought to still be playing with me as in olden times.

   Freddie (Fred Bennett) says it looks mighty suspicious for you to go to American Falls. Guess he thinks you will send for me like Don did for Hilma, but you wouldn't do it love and I wouldn't not come to you if you did. That sounds so nice that you are coming back to leave me – never again.

   A year ago today sweetheart Don and Hilma visited us at Cedar Creek and a year ago tomorrow night –then what happened? I was sick coming home. O my precious love how frightened you were.

   (Agnes to Robert) ...*That sounds so nice that you are coming back to leave me – never again. I have been singing "Never Alone" It sounds sad and yet I am not alone as I would be if you were not "mine"...*

   (Agnes to Robert) ...*My heart cries for you to come back, but I want you to have a nice long visit with your father and get to know him again...*

(Robert to Agnes) *I have and am now, wearing my pretty shirt and pink necktie that you made for me, Dearest and I like them cause 'em is pretty. The shirt collar is big enough, just right. Mrs. Bennett asked me where I got this shirt and I told her Sears and Roebuck.*

(Agnes to Robert) *... Only this morning I wrote you, dear heart, and see what a lot I must say. I am glad one day is gone, only six more days till I can see you again.*

(Agnes to Robert) *...Have a good time my darling and remember to be my <u>good boy</u>. I am happy I have your sweet face to kiss in a picture. Good night God Bless you, yours with unchanging love Agnes.*

(Robert to Agnes) *....You said you were going to the dance, that will be good sweetheart. Is Mamie Just going too? If she isn't we will go, horseback, won't we? If we go in the cutter you will have to drive because Daddy Just will be afraid I will drive the horses too fast. Don't you think so? I remain your Darling boy lover forever, Rufus"*

(Robert to Agnes) *How is Mama Just, is she well these days? Dear, I hope she is. God Bless her, cause she is so good and we love her don't we, Darling?*

(Robert to Agnes) *I got your letter this morning you ask if I was sad the other morning when I left there. Yes, I was Darling, I would have stayed longer, but I was afraid I would cry, it was all I could do to keep the tears from coming to my eyes, while I sat on the wood box. I think I am a kind of silly kid, don't you?*

(Robert to Agnes and Emma in Boise) ...... *"Dear little girl and mama"* and another *"Dear wife and mama"*. Letter was addressed Agnes Just, Boise General Delivery.

Bob and Agnes were married by a Justice of the Peace at the Doll Baird home, then in Springfield, Idaho. The wedding date was Nov 28, 1906. Mimi was 19 and Bob was 22. After the ceremony, they returned for a wedding dinner at the Just home with another couple, the Sages, who were married the same day. Among Mimi's mementos are the wedding write up from the Shelley Pioneer and a piece of wallpaper from the room in which they were wed. I don't know why there isn't a picture of them in their wedding attire. Agnes's older brothers, Jim and Charlie both have formal photos of their weddings.

Two letters from James Reid about Robert and Mimi's wedding

Dec 1, 06
My Dear Son I received your letter on Wednesday and was very glad to hear you are well and working. I admit that I neglected answering your letter too long but it was just neglect. You tell me you are married I was not much surprised to hear it but I don't know whether you should have married or not. You will find that your troubles begin then but I hope your joys are many and your happiness complete. I have had a great deal of trouble in my life but I trust that you will never have to undergo what I have had to.

………. Well, I suppose by this time you are married have you any idea what you have done, I don't believe you have, but I am in hopes that you will prove yourself to be a man and be to her, a husband. Remember, she has left an exceptionally good home for you; therefore, you must do your very best for her and always remember that she is your equal and counselor in respect and all occasions so now I will close wishing you a long, happy and prosperous life and may God Bless you, my children.

I am your father, James Reid.
P. S. While writing I have read notice from Mr. Just of your marriage.   J R

  (In a letter, soon after) *P. S. I am very sorry if I said anything in my last letter to cause you any sadness and hope you will not grieve over it very much. Just put it down to the ramblings of an old fool. I am sure I forgive the little girl for taking my boy, I guess she has far more legal claim to him now, than I ever had. Someday I may see you and explain that mistake I spoke of. So now good bye and God bless you both. Regards to Mr. and Mrs. Just.*

Write soon, Your Father

Dec 06 (Jim, Robert's brother wrote after he hears of the wedding) *"Dear brother and sister……Well Brother, it seems easy, but it ain't."* In the same envelope is a letter from Jim's wife, Lymeda, congratulating them both!

This shot was taken soon after they were married. Robert is on Monte, Mimi on Blue. The description of the picture says Blue Dog. Surely it's the same horse, but I have never heard the "dog" before.

One More Ride
I'd like to have one more ride with you,
You ride Monte and I ride Blue.
We'd go to the top of yon mountain peak,
We might ride miles and never speak,
But we'd find a kinship rare and true
While you rode Monte and I rode Blue.

We'd stop at the creek and get a drink,
Rest a while 'neath a birch and think,
We'd quote some verses or hum a song,
Fitting things, as we jog along,
We'd watch the sunset and feel the dew
While you rode Monte and I rode Blue.
                         By Agnes Just Reid
                         Rugged Rhymes, published 1947

Children of Robert and Agnes

Eldro Just (El) Reid
Oct 7, 1910 - Sept 1, 1993

Married Geraldine Larsen
June 5, 1930

Children

Eldro Jay	August 28, 1936 - August 28,1936	
Katherine	Oct 19, 1937 - Aug 3, 2021	Married Leonard Spraker children: Steven, Julie, Lisa, Linda, Philip
Caroline	Oct 19, 1937 - Aug 15, 2018	Married Don Aikele children: Bret, Gina, Teresa, Donna, Valerie

Jerrie was never called Geraldine by the Reids, and she spelled her name several different ways. They were childless for many years. The infertility problem was cured by an operation and Jerrie got pregnant. She had a horrible delivery in the hospital in Idaho Falls, the baby (Eldro Jay) was about 10 lbs. and should have been delivered caesarian. It was too hard on the baby and he died about 10 hours later.

Luckily Jerrie got pregnant again in about 6 months and had identical twins Katherine and Caroline with beautiful curly red hair.

(Mimi wrote) *When we were leaving (to have El) my mother was getting dressed to go with us and I told her she was most unwelcome. She said; "What will you do if the baby is born on the way? I said, "If I happen to have that good luck, I'll still have strength to take care of him." He was born eight hours later and the instruments were all sterilized ready to use and my strength was at a mighty low ebb. When we got to the hospital we had to go upstairs and I thought the doctor and my husband would surely carry me. I was so sick and not as heavy as I am now. Those two unfeeling men made me walk up those stairs.*

(Gwen wrote) *Eldro was the first born of the five boys. He was born in Shelley, in the little room provided in the doctor's home. His four brothers were all born in the home on the Blackfoot River site.*

(Gwen wrote) *I wonder if you know the story about "Cago." Agnes and Bob had friends (the Spauldings) in Chicago, who sent this little very real looking rocking horse to Eldro. Since it came from Chicago and Eldro could not say the whole word, he called it "Cago." Cago has probably had more riders and lived longer than any horse in the world.*

The wooden rocking horse was covered with a pinto horse hide when he came and the Reid boys all rode him. Robert covered him with a black horse hide when the pinto one was worn off. In turn the black one wore off and Don Reid covered him in another pinto hide that he has now. We grandchildren remembered him being in the hall but we weren't allowed to ride him. Since it was given to Eldro, it lived at his house for many years. He was returned back to the old house when El and Jerrie died.

(Gwen wrote) *At one time Bob and Agnes patiently, but persistently, worked for months with their son, Eldro, who was afflicted with polio, and the boy recovered completely.* Mimi memorialized this subject many times, this is only one version.

His Health

Big boy had always been an especially sturdy child. He was the pride of our lives when he weighed thirty-one pounds at nine months old. Since then it has been discovered that babies have no business carrying so much extra weight, but in those days ignorance was indeed bliss. He was well and we thought he was perfect in every way, so life was full of bliss for us.

Early in life he had whooping cough and measles as all well-regulated children should, or usually do. Then the spring after he was ten years old, he developed a very serious malady. He had complained that his head ached but he was subject to headaches and we did not give it thought except that I always kept a fever thermometer in the house and I took his temperature finding it normal. The next morning when he tried to dress himself, he fell over. He was alone so when he told me, I supposed he was a little dizzy and gave it no thought. He seemed perfectly well but several times during the day he would fall over as soon as he was off center. The next morning, he was losing the use of his legs so that he fell over almost constantly and his arms were not real *dependable and he experienced difficulty in swallowing so we began to realize that it was paralysis.*

We talked to our family doctor but he said it looked like a case for a chiropractor so the next day we took him to the nearest one. Spring was just breaking and the roads were so bad that we could not run cars so we started to the nearest point on the railroad seven miles away, to catch the train. We had to leave the two smaller boys with my mother who was over seventy and in poor health, and go forth, we knew not where nor of what avail. We jiggled along in a big farm wagon with the faithful old team that were like members of the family and I don't ever remember a sadder day in all our 24 years of married life. As so often happens on cold spring days, great flocks of blue birds were along the road and they kept following us lifting daintily on the fence posts until we got very near. There followed many weary days though, when there was nothing that held out much hope. The chiropractor soon told us he could not help him and we could see he was getting worse every minute. He soon had to be carried and he was a big ten-year-old for his daddy to lift and if his head drooped back a little, he would lose control of it, so that it would wobble around like an idiotic child. There was just one consolation. Though he could not feed himself, his mind was not affected, neither was his speech. Daddy and I spent all of our time reading to him and amusing him any way we could.

The chiropractor finally advised us to go to another town where a clinic was being held and have him examined. Ten or twelve doctors from over the state looked at him questioned him and shook their heads. It was new to them all. One said he thought he had seen a similar case in Germany, but never anything like it on this side of the water. Anyway, they kept him at the hospital for observations but it was plain that they were working in the dark. Another thing the mental effect of people suffering and people dying and the rebellious longing to go home were doing him more harm than any treatment could do him good. In less than a week they concluded to give up the case and let us bring him home. They said that home nursing might do better than anything.

. . .There was one doctor who had said, "Well it came on gradually and I think it will gradually pass away." Like the sight of the blue birds, that was our ray of hope.

The home nursing became mostly a school of discipline and I shall always believe that his daddy's untiring efforts are what saved him from spending his life in a wheel chair. Friends of ours had a somewhat similar experience, the husband and father stricken down while strong and robust to spend years in a wheel chair because of an attack of infantile paralysis. I talked to the wife about it and she said Big Boy's symptoms were identical with his. I was ready to bow to the inevitable, but not Daddy. A Scotchman is not that easily whipped. For hours, each day he stood over that boy massaging his limbs and making him use them. He'd say almost harshly' "straighten that foot out" "Pull that foot back" "lift up that hand." Big Boy would whimper and cry and declare that he could not, but Daddy would keep at him till he did. Then so gradually that we hardly knew it, he began to get better and on Easter Sunday, oh was there ever such a glorious Easter, he walked a few faltering steps.

Nature would not have permitted any more delay in the recovery for already his muscles were wasting away so fast that there would soon have been nothing left to function. I told him often that Nature cured him and once he said "Mama when it was spring and Nature was busy making the grass grow and leaves came out on the trees, how could she have time to come in the house and make me well?" Perhaps it was because such a good Catholic friend of the family had mass said for him in a distant city, perhaps it was because a little girl with big braids of reddish hair prayed for him every night. Whatever the cause of his recovery, I still have a heart fairly bursting with gratitude. His Mother

The family was instructed to make El get up by himself if he fell, to strengthen his muscles. It was hard for them to see El crawl to a fence to get himself upright.

(Gwen wrote) *El and Vin were buddies, and often went to the hills with their dad to tend cattle, mend fences or to visit some of their Dad's relatives who had homesteads there. Eldro loved to work, did chores at home, milked cows, broke horses. Eldro cannot be described in a short story. He was too great a person to tell about his personality, his accomplishments, his love of his family, for Jerrie, his daughters, grand and great grand kids. Also love of the hills.*

Eldro was fast at cutting horns off cattle.

Eldro and Jerrie went to school together and were always boy and girl friends. The Larsens were great friends, despite them being staunch Mormons and the Reids practicing no religion.

Eldro was known to take the best piece of meat from the platter and even steal the heart of the watermelon you were saving for last.

Eldro liked to use "puffed up" when someone was exceedingly proud of himself. Butch was Fred's nickname for Eldro.

(Mimi wrote) *Oh, how I wish my dad had stayed in the Mormon Church so I'd have been born one and it may be the simplest way out of it, to join now. I can't go through this for more times and live.*

(Jerrie wrote to Mimi about her parents and upcoming marriage) *I fear and tremble when I think of the way my folks will take it when I tell them I'm to be married in June. I've told them before but they don't believe. I must really talk to them sometime soon. I followed mother all over the house last night trying, trying to get the courage.*

(Jerrie wrote) *The day we got the ring, Mr. Christ almost cried when he wished us happiness. He looked and sounded so sincere. He said he knew of no two whom he would rather wish good fortune. Then with his eyes rather shinier than natural and his face more red. He added "I mean it, honestly."*

Jerrie wrote that she felt very fortunate to marry into a family who had so many nice friends.

(Jerrie wrote) *The most fun I've had during the round-up was the ride with Mr. Reid up on the hills east of Paradise. He's the dearest man.*

After Jerrie and El were married, they lived in the valley for about seven years. I think they were happy, Jerrie gave no hint that she was unhappy about the arrangement. They wanted to live in a permanent home on land of their own. It was too expensive to buy the machinery and horses for their own place.

(Gwen wrote) *Jerrie and Eldro lived in the Bennett home and boarded teachers for the Lower Presto School. Eldro had hopes he could buy the farm when it would be for sale. The Bennett boys did not want to farm. They wanted to go to California and wanted instant money when the farm was sold. Eldro did not have instant money and his parents were not able to help.*

When Alvin Just's wife Dora died, and he married Mary Grange, she came with money so Alvin and Mary could pay cash for the Bennett place.

Jerrie and El then moved into the little white house across the lane from Bob and Agnes. They were planning on building a home, bought the logs and had the basement dug in the lower field by Chick Just's house. The hole is still there. Winter came and they were unable to start construction.

(Mimi wrote) *Maybe some time, it will seem pleasanter, but just now it seems as if we are all forced to do what we do not want to do. I hate to have the kids back here because I know they'd rather be farther away, but it is out of the question for them to rent or buy a place at any distance for it would mean a small fortune put up for horses and machinery.*

I know the family knew Jerrie wasn't satisfied with the move to the little white house and when they couldn't start the house in the lower field, El needed to find someplace to pacify Jerrie, and the place in Firth was found.

(Mimi wrote) *Jerrie and Eldro had twin girls born October 19 and are we a happy family! What could ever have happened to the Reid family that could be so satisfying. After all these years of praying for a girl baby, we have two at once. They were premature but are doing well now. They weighed 4 pounds 4 ounces each at birth, but now they weigh nearly seven and such perfect babies. At first, they did not look alike but now we cannot tell them apart. Oh, how we love 'em.*

(Mimi wrote about Grandy) *He is making another nursery chair for Jerrie. She had one that her mother had given her and one that Daddy had made and she found out which was best so he is making this one to order.*

(Mimi wrote when Jerrie brought the twins over for Mother's Day). *Rufus held them both at once and rocked them and told them he was going to bring home a wood tick for each of them next time he goes to the hills.*

(Gwen wrote) *After much searching, they found what they were looking for, a home (i*t was a beautiful 2-story home and yard with big poplars.) *and some farm ground. The land was divided by canals by the Snake River, and was not enough to make a good living and that was the start of the dairy business. It was not Eldro's choice, but it was successful. He took many honors for his dairy cattle.*

Being a dairy farmer is a full-time job, so times with them were rare. Jerrie taught school several years at Lavaside and Firth.

Eldro had started to prove up on some land in the hills, but he gave that up when he bought the house and acreage.

(Gwen wrote) *Eldro had many helpers who adored him and some of them say he made them who they are today. He was fair, he was honest, he was their friend. This is one of my favorite stories. When he was old enough to get social security, he was given a choice. If he was making a certain amount of money, he could not take Social Security until later. Checks came every month. He simply put them away in a big drawer unopened. Some years later the IRS came and informed him he had been getting Social Security checks illegally and had to pay back every penny. Eldro simply took the drawer and dumped all the envelopes in front of him. That embarrassed fellow was so bewildered it took him all day to get things right and Eldro had the last laugh.*

Dad remembered one time El, Jerrie and the twins, came riding their horses from Firth to the home place for a visit.

Jerrie wrote lots of letters to Mimi, as unmarried, newly married and as new parents of the twins. In them she expresses how she loves the Reids. I am sure Mimi and Grandy and the brothers would have never suspected how estranged they would be after the move to Firth.

Jerrie was intent on Eldro becoming a member of the Mormon church. Eldro promised Florence, Jerrie's mother, that he would be baptized when he turned 65. He kept this promise. After that, the Reids saw even less of him. Jerrie kept a tight rein on all of Eldro's activity. He would always have to be home at a designated hour, so even if the brothers saw him, he had to hurry home. When anyone asked if they could come for a visit, Jerrie would tell them she was ill. Doug said that Mimi visited without notice, but it was always strained, and never as often as she wanted. Mimi knew Jerrie loved El and El loved Jerrie.

(Mimi wrote) in her diary, October 19, 1943. *Eldro has only been here once since May.*

We very seldom saw the two of them at any family functions but it was a real treat when they did come. Jerrie was a beautiful, red-haired woman and we thought she was lovely. El was so dapper with his mustache. We loved the other brothers so much, we knew we would love him too.

Jerrie had taught Dad at school. She boarded with her folks just across the field from the school. Mimi said Jerrie and El used Dad to carry letters back and forth.

Many years later she was Fred's son Rich's teacher.

She wrote:

Dearest Mimi, how wonderful it is to have a boy bring a note from you to me at the school again! Isn't it amazing how things turn out? When I finished that year back in '30 I was so certain that I'd never teach again. Now, I am teaching the son of the boy who used to bring me love letters from my precious Eldro and his mother.... What a smile Janene had on her pretty face (oh isn't it!) when she saw me Monday morning, too. Its bright sweetness burned away all my doubts and fears and it is fun to teach Rich he is so quick and intelligent.

Mimi had saved lots of beautiful Mother's Day and birthday cards from Jerrie. The letters stopped, or at least weren't saved, until the above letter.

After growing up together, working side by side for all those years, to be so close, yet so out of reach, was heart wrenching for the family. We saw the rare times when El was there, the men were almost giddy with excitement. The other brothers continued to work together, harvesting crops and working cattle. We kids felt cheated that we didn't get to know El and his family like the other brothers and their families. The brothers felt cheated of all the laughter and visiting, and Grandy and Mimi were cheated of the time and love of their oldest son and their beloved granddaughters. And worst of all, El had to endure the pain of knowing he had to choose his wife over his family. Hopefully the days are past that religion comes between loving families.

Robert Vincent
June 30, 1914 - Feb 3, 2009

Married Gwen Davis
June 3, 1936

Children

Barbara Jane	Dec 25, 1941- April 12, 2023	Married Roger Hanson – children: Stacey, Reid
Robert Edward	March 16, 1944	Married Christy Crockett – children: Katie, Mindi, Cody, Robert, Jared
Ted Vincent	June 21, 1946-July 11, 1998	Married Debbie Bowne, divorced
Paul Eldon	June 22, 1948	Married Billie Ann Shikashio – children: Milee, Mariko, Kimi
William Davis (Bill)	Aug 24, 1951	Married Donetta Harris – children: Melissa, Brittany
Gerry Anne	Jan 25, 1954	Married Bill Becker (deceased) – children: Ben, Andy, Emily Married Dan Cummins
Virginia Rae (Ginger)	Aug 23, 1955	

(Mimi wrote) *Eldro carried a tiny thimble around for a long-time telling folks it was for "my little sister." I can remember him showing it to Jim Just and he was quite embarrassed. The little sister proved to be Vin.*

Someone told Vin when he was a little guy, that he looked like his mother. He responded, "*I must be ugly!*" Mimi thought that was funny and told it on him as long as she lived. She thought he must have wanted to look like his father since he was a boy.

Excerpts from Vin's story about his Dad

My dad was especially good at being our father. The thing I loved best about Dad was how he always had time for us. Dad showed us about life by his actions and his love. We worked together and played together. Dad taught me by word or example, everything I know. He was always so gentle and he was always fair. He never promoted himself and he wasn't aggressive but he didn't let people push him either. He taught me how to milk the cows, ride and care for the horses, how work was necessary and how to be a responsible worker. I loved to hear him sing and whistle and I wanted to be just like him.

Dad was tolerant but straightened me out when I did something wrong. I never did have much trouble with discipline, I was a model child you know. One time, when I was 9 or 10, I was misbehaving, so Dad made me get out of the car and made me walk home. It would have been about a mile, and I decided to worry my folks by not going home. Of course, they came after me so that was a joke on them.

There was one other time, I guess, when Fred was about three or four, I suppose, he had a little fire engine, with horses on it that he would pull up and down the kitchen for entertainment. And he'd do it - - - by the hour. In our house, we had a little corner between the flour box and the big stove that was kind of a shelter that we liked because it was warm, always, and we used to put overshoes in that corner to keep warm. So, Fred was having his parade, one night and I was in this corner staying warm and, so when Fred would go by, I'd kick an overshoe out there and tip his outfit over. And he'd - - - bawl of course. But anyway, it went on for two or three trips. I don't remember that Dad ever told me to cut it out or not, but anyway he finally got tired of it and got up and got me by the hair and led me to that old big hall that was colder than zero. Shut the door on me and said, "Come out when you are ready to behave." So, that was the only occasion I ever "did time."

When we were kids, we would go with dad a lot more than he wanted us to go – in the wintertime. We would insist on going with him to feed the cattle and we'd bawl all the way, he said, because we would freeze. We would put our little coaster sleighs behind the big sleigh but we'd fall off and he'd have to stop and wait for us so it would take him too long to feed. But we always got to go unless it was below zero.

Dad never indicated he wanted me to be anything other than who I was. My mom once told me I had a "surgeon's hand", but that never was one of my goals. My dad was my example to learn right from wrong. He expected all us boys to be our best, do our best, and live right. My parents made our house a home by their love for us. They were there, always. We worked, laughed, ate, and played as a family. My mom and dad showed more love for each other and us boys than any family I ever knew.

Vin and Roy (Buck) Bower rode together on the same horse to school. When they arrived at the school, Vin found his grade was having the day off. How to get home? Roy would need the horse to return in the afternoon. Vin knew his family was to be in the hills that day so he took the saddle off the horse and carried it the three miles home. He put the saddle on another horse and took off for the hills. That left Roy the horse to ride home, but he had to ride bareback.

(Mimi wrote) *Another thing. I fear Vin is a born "ladies' man" he can wear someone's old left over suit and look like a million dollars and without being in the least aggressive, can smile that "come hither" smile that brings the girls his way. Up to the present he has always been wise in his choice of girls to whom he sends valentines...Vin is altogether too popular. He dances too well and is too good looking. I realize now that I should have considered all these things when I selected a dad for him and picked out a good ugly one.*

Gwen was visiting a friend in Idaho Falls. She had graduated with her teaching certificate but hadn't found a job. She wanted to stay close to home in Aberdeen. A friend of hers had already applied and got the job for Lower Presto. Gwen's father contacted her in Idaho Falls, and said her friend had decided to turn down the Lower Presto job and she WOULD go to apply on her way home to Aberdeen. Gwen was shy and sure she didn't want to do that, but her father was firm. Gwen went by and visited with Frank Pratt, one of the school board members. She was informed that Robert Reid was at a funeral (Hilma's) and couldn't interview her. She got the job much to her chagrin.

When she arrived at the Reid house where she would be staying, she and Blanche Pratt made themselves at home because Blanche was already living there and no one was home. Mimi and El arrived before they went to bed, so Gwen met them. When she woke in the morning Mimi introduced her to another son. Gwen said, "I met him last night." "No," Mimi said, "this is another Vin."

Gwen immediately felt loved when she met the Reid family.

She shared the small bedroom closest to the porch with Blanche Pratt. They each had one drawer for their clothes plus some hooks on the wall. They would clean up by washing from a basin of warm water from the fire Robert had started. The teachers slept in Grandy and Mimi's house, but would take their meals at Eldro and Jerrie's across the road. Gwen taught Wallace and Doug. She soon fell for Vin and only taught the one year. In those days teachers couldn't be married and still hold their job.

(Gwen wrote) *I was the lucky one as a teacher who boarded with Eldro and Jerrie in the little white house across the road from the senior Reids. Yes, we were furnished Eldro's little rumble-seat car, filled with gas for transportation to and from school when the weather was nice.*

In the winter it was a glorious sleigh ride tucked under blankets watching Vin and Fred skiing behind. Leaving the teachers and Doug and Wallace at the schoolhouse, the boys would go after hay for their cattle back home, feed the cattle then return to the school to take us all home. After supper, we would play games or just visit.

(Mimi wrote) *Gwen came to teach at the Presto School and stayed…They had a wedding shower for Gwen, and honestly, they got everything but the house and auto.*

Gwen told me the story of their honeymoon. After the wedding they were heading to Kittie and Ed Blair's homestead cabin in the hills. Aunt Kit had given them two roosters so they could have a nice chicken dinner during their stay. They were in a little cage in the rumble seat of the car. The road was bad from a recent storm so they had to backtrack and stay the night in a motel in Blackfoot. She laughed telling the story of waking up to loud cock-a-doodle-doos and the rush to try the road again in the early dawn.

After Gwen and Vin were married, Grandy and Mimi paid to get her teeth fixed. Gwen was embarrassed, but her family was not financially able to fix them. The dentist ground them down and put on permanent caps. She used these same teeth as long as she lived. Mimi and Grandy gave her a beautiful blue velvet dress.

(Mimi wrote) *Vin and Gwen are having a baby around Christmas time! We are happy beyond words. I was just getting so worried for fear Vin, who loves babies more than anyone of our family, was never to have one of his own. Now they are going to. Gwen really is wonderful help to all of us. She helps me then rushes over to do something for Jerrie. Oh, she is a lovely, sunny girl! Don't see yet how we happened to get such superior girls. It is much better than having them on my own. Some other mother trained them so perfectly, then gave me the finished product without cost or obligation. I think Rufus is going to enjoy Gwen a lot. Yesterday he took her for her very first horseback ride and they picked currants all morning together. She and Jerrie are very fond of each other and she has always made a hit with Eldro, and Fred plays with her so much, and the little boys adore her, so take it all around, I think the whole family is pleased.*

Vin and Gwen used Eldro's logs to build their home that sat north of the iron fence, where the old shop stands now. The 2-room log house was moved in Oct, 1941 to the present location about a mile west on the old Charlie and Bertha Just site. They hired "Happy the Mover" from Idaho Falls. They moved a 20' X 26' log home including a

4' X 12' porch for $150.00. Vin's hat was still hanging on its hook and no dishes were disturbed in the cupboards. Santa found their new location and on Christmas day brought baby Barbara.

(Mimi wrote about Gwen) *You should have talked to my son's wife or listened in when she was delivering a gift to the bride. It goes like this: "You think you love him now, but wait until you have been married a year, then you'll know what love is," or "Wait until you have been married ten years and you'll know what love is." The time has stretched now to thirty-five years but the advice is still the same…Gwen said life goes by so fast. How can I ever get done all the things I want to? See all the things I want to see? Learn all the things I want to learn?*

Fred Bennett
Feb 25, 1919 - April 20, 2013

Married Alma Jemmett
Dec 27, 1942

Children

Fred Richard	June 17, 1945	Married Charlotte Hughes– children: Jill, Jess, Carson
Alma Janene	May 24, 1947	Married Jim Cotton – children: Brent, Clint, Ladd, Adam
Donna Lois	June 26, 1950	Married Jay Horkley, divorced Married Todd Neuenschwander, divorced Married Bob McWilliams – stepchildren: Richard, Caroline
Merle Jo	Aug 30, 1952	Married Jack Clark – children: Ace, Cole, Sage, Ott
Becky Lou	May 29, 1956	Married Ken Davis – children: Megan, Zach
Kittie Sue	Dec 9, 1957	Married Steve Peterson – children: Lex, Trevor, Hans, Cooper
Wendy Kay	July 26, 1959	Married Tom Ritter – child: Callie, divorced Married Mark Pratt – children: Seth, Anna

(Grandy wrote in Portland about Rich) *Got your letter and the picture of the little Codger. He is a husky little brat, isn't he? I can't see that he resembles anyone except another baby about as fat and old as he is.*

This was in a tablet to Eldro by Mimi

Freddie
You will remember how daddy called you and Vincent both out of Gaggy's room one morning in winter time and brought you into the big room. How you both tip-toed and grinning just like you thought Santa Claus had been here. Then Daddy took you to look into a basket and there you found Freddie. Not a little sister but Freddie, little brother Freddie. Vincent looked at him and then whispered to you "He ain't dry yet." All his hair was plastered down with oil that the nurse had put on and Vincent did not know what to think. You've often remembered since "And Mama talked to us, I thought she'd be sick but she talked." Such happy little boys to have a brother. "Little black head," "My little blackie," "Kiss, kiss my little black head."

Grandy delivered Dad. They saw the lights of the doctor's car approaching but he didn't quite make it. Dad weighed about 11 lbs.

Freda, Fred Twitchell's daughter was there to help Mimi after Dad was born. DeLoris Henscheid took Freda, her mother, up to see Fred and Alma before she died. Freda told Dad that she had changed his diapers.

(Mimi wrote) *We started Fred camping when he was 1-year-old. That is why he is so nice.*

(Mimi wrote) *When Fred was about four, I was joking to their dad about a few chest hairs that showed over his open collar. I called them his turkey whiskers. The little guy went over to his dad and put his arms around him defensively saying 'I'd love him even if he was covered with hair.' That is love and it does not demand polished shoes and a pressed suit.*

Dad was helping Grandy pitch hay in the lower field; it was grass hay and too short to get much of a fork full. He was working hard and felt like he was doing a good job. His dad said, "get out of the way you little prune and let me get some work done." Dad said he "melted right there in the grass in a heap."

Dad's best friends while going to school were Steve Phillips, Hank Williams and Allan (Bus) Larsen. Allan lived at the Larsen place by the school. Dad said it wasn't far on a horse.

Fred loved going barefoot. El told of a time he saw him about 12-yrs-old, driving a team raking hay in the early fall. Dad had on his hat and overcoat but was barefoot.

Fred 's favorite job was driving a team of horses.

Dora always said she hoped her boys would be like Fred Reid.

Fred Reid in the Army:

Alma's mother Daphne Jemmett kept a newsletter, The Alridge Chronical, to and about the soldiers that were serving during the war. She had 3 sons, a brother-in-law and Fred, her son in law, as well as lots of neighbors and friends serving in various places.

Fred and Alma were married about 2 ½ years when Dad was drafted. (Mimi wrote) *Uncle Sam called Fred on New Year's.* She had philosophies of peace at all costs. They tried to get Dad released from the army when Grandy was in poor health and a ranch to run. Mimi wrote to my Mom and Dad when she was resigned to the inevitable. *You are named after the right man, Fred. That was Fred Bennett's philosophy. "Never begin anything that you can't finish." . . . As always, Dad and I feel just alike about it. We'll get along even if we don't make much money.*

(Mimi wrote at this time) *I too hope that Fred need not go to the far away army posts. True, there is more chance of their coming back uninjured, but the break in their lives is just as hard to bridge – possibly harder, than when the fighting was heaviest. You have always had your sons close, so long a part of your family, the pain of letting them go is just that much greater.*

I hope Fred's little son looks exactly like him, and learns to smile with that irresistible winsomeness not often found. There is no greater wish I can make for that little one than that he be endowed with the gentleness, the firmness, the kindness and the justice shown by his father.

Dad met Allan Thompson in Salt Lake City when they were inducted into the army. Allan knew the Reid name as Bill and Dick had homesteads near him. When he heard Reid called, he struck up a conversation with Dad, and so began a life-long friendship.

(Mimi wrote in 1950) *Allan Thompson made a talk at church or mutual and used Fred as a model for all LDS boys to follow.*

They stayed at Salt Lake for 3 or 4 days and then off to Fort Hood, Texas.

(Mimi wrote) They *drafted our son who had run the place from the time his father was stricken. The two older boys were on farms of their own, the two younger ones were little boys. My husband was at Portland taking treatments on the last lap of an eight-year journey to find health. Fred went in May. His son was born three weeks later. We had no way to reach him. He had just been transferred to Camp Hood. We didn't raise very good crops that year but we did raise a fine baby.* Dad got a telegram that said the baby was fine. He worried that meant that Alma wasn't.

(Fred wrote) *Dear Iris and Chick,*

You were right Iris, I was glad to get your unbiased opinion of my new son and heir…We've had quite a lot of close order drills and some long marches but we need quite a lot more I think. So, do the officers. We had rifle inspection yesterday and no one in our platoon passed it.

*It's raining here tonight, it makes it quite a lot cooler. It gets awfully muddy here when it rains, your feet ball up till you can't lift them and boy do we dirty up the barracks...We have physical training almost every day. We have numerous exercises and end up by going 7 parts at double time to 1-part quick time. Lots of guys fall out poor cusses...They asked me what my hobby was in the classification room today and I told them we worked in our spare time where I came from. (*He finally put down horseback riding.*) They're really a great bunch down here in Texas.*

Dad was in the army for most of the time Grandy was in Portland in an attempt to help his asthma. Dad wrote him often and wrote also to the family at home, where Alma was staying. Both Grandy and Mimi would include the letters Fred had written to them when they wrote back and forth.

(Fred wrote) *We got as wet as a drowned rat the other day twice, once in the morning, once in the afternoon. We had to walk in a muddy water filled gully about waist deep coming in. Felt just like the infantry then. Had pork chops and brown gravy and ice cream for dinner. Did I tell you how much I made last month? I got $14.40, quite a lot huh?*

...We've had quite a lot of training in concealment of man and material this week. Some practice and some classes. We've also had some more first aid practice. Me and another guy got called out in front of the Co. to treat a man who was supposed to have been hit with shrapnel. He had a compound fracture above the elbow and was bleeding from a large artery. Well, we treated him up, put a tourniquet on him and bandaged him up. We didn't do too good or too bad I guess; I suppose he'd have been a gone gosling tho if he'd really been hurt.

Well, I sure hope you're feeling good dad. Lots of love from Fred

(Grandy wrote) *I try to write to Fred every day or two to let him know how I am. He worries so about me it seems. He is such a good old Fred kid.*

Fred was on training Texas when they were all called together and the Sarge announced that Truman had dropped the Hiroshima Bomb on Japan and "it packed a wallop." Japan surrendered a few days later. Dad thought they didn't surrender right away and the second bomb convinced them. He thought the bombs were horrid, but if American troops had needed to go through Japan, it would have killed many more on both sides.

Fred wasn't released yet though. He finished training in Texas and went on to Georgia. Alma and 6-month-old Rich, and Allan Thompson's wife, Lorene, and their 1-year-old daughter, Sharon, took the train together. They left in December, sometime before Christmas. Mom was train sick a lot; Rich was cranky and spit up constantly. But it was wonderful when they got there.

Mom and Dad lived in Georgia for about a year. (Alma wrote) *I really had a good time in Georgia with my little boy and Fred all to myself when he was home.*

This photo is of Fred, Rich and Alma. They lived 10 or 15 miles from the army base. Dad rode the bus with his friend Turk, Richard V. Turknet. Turk's nickname for Fred was "Idaho." When Dad was discharged, Turk loaded all their belongings in his car and took them to catch the train home. Fred remembers with misgivings that he didn't ever write to him. Dad said, "The war was over and everyone just got busy with life." Fred honored Turk by naming several horses after him.

Stuart Portela, an instructor and coach at Firth High School, was instrumental in honoring veterans from the Firth area of the World War II era that were in the service and unable to graduate with their classmates. There was a national movement to get these veterans their diplomas. Dad graduated with my daughter Sage's high school class at Firth in 2002. Ronald Hughes, Jim Mattson, Steve and Mark Phillips, among others, received their diplomas as well.

Miscarried baby

Doug said, Mimi always said she probably missed her chance for a girl.

(Mimi wrote) *Frances is one of the names that was waiting for my daughter, and I just missed having it myself for it was my grandmother's name.*

Douglass James
Sept 11, 1926 - May 13, 2012

(Mimi wrote) *Dougie is a born gardener. But I think it will develop more along decorative lines. Flowers just take his breath.*

(Mimi wrote when she was sick in bed.) *Dougie did all my work. Eldro brought the babies over so he had nine for dinner and Gwen was at Aberdeen so he took over the house. He brought me the daintiest meals to my bedside. He loves to do those things so I guess I need not grieve for a girl I never had.*

(Mimi wrote about Doug making a card for her birthday on Mother's Day) *"Dear Mom: You are a yellow rose. You are a golden poppy." I showed it to the older woman I was visiting, a friend. I said, 'Is he going to be a poet?' With tears filling her big eyes she answered, 'He is a poet.' So, it is nice that it worked out for him to take care of me all these years. Not much of a life for him but surely wonderful for me.*

(Mimi wrote) *One of my happiest recollections is of the time I watched our very blond son and a Japanese boy bend over the same task in third grade in our little unconsolidated country school. Just the two of them and what a pair they were. Not a bit of difference in their intelligence, just their coloring.*

He has one of the leading parts in the all-school play, and is to have a new suit so he is quite a changed Dougie...Doug is the one that looks just like his father. The others are more like him in their actions but Doug has the same handsome blond face.

...Doug has such gorgeous flowers. I wish everyone could come see them before there is a frost. It seemed to me he was always trying different varieties and different places to plant. One of our favorites was clematis on the porch of the old house. He had

strung sisal baling string in a fan pattern from the support posts and they were covered with purple blossoms.

...He is a newspaper man, not a cowboy. He does not wear big hats. In fact, he has never owned a hat in all his thirty-three years.

Doug and a friend put out a newspaper in Firth. It must have had a weekly printing. There are a few copies, one is telling of the 5-year anniversary.

Doug was valedictorian of his graduating class and gave his speech on Franklin Delano Roosevelt. Mimi was in Portland with Grandy. Doug was proud he had written the speech all by himself.

(Grandy wrote in a letter) *Doug was called for the army in December but did not pass for some reason, we never did find out why.*

Mimi thought shovels would be a good Christmas gift for the women of the family that were always looking for a shovel to irrigate their gardens. So Doug decided to wrap them so that no one would ever guess. He is an expert at the art of gift wrapping. He made them look like huge candles. (Mimi wrote) *if the angels in heaven wanted packages wrapped, I'm sure they'd employ Doug. The first step was a special trip to town to buy two lengths of stove pipe to transform the shovel handles into candles then he covered each one with red tissue and wound tinsel around in an artistic manner and set a yellow flame on top.*

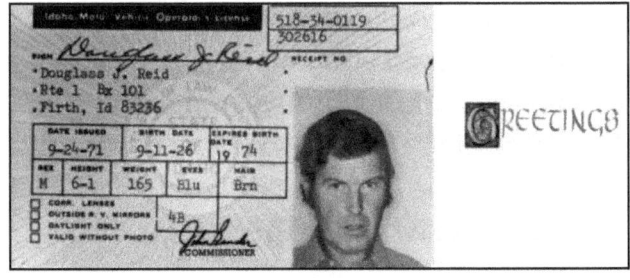

Doug always had an inventive Christmas card. One year he used his driver's license with greetings added!

(Mimi wrote) *We have a son 26 who has been two years with one of our biggest newspapers in the west. With a merger, a short time ago, he lost out. Everyone says he had what it takes to become a brilliant newspaper man. He had a yen for writing from the day he was born, but he is not interested in any job that would take him away from the valley where he was born, so that's his business. If he prefers to raise chickens and flowers, who am I to urge newspaper work? He had decided this is where I belong.*

(Mimi wrote in a letter to Carl Hagen about Doug) *He has always been very companionable to me so the natural conclusion is that he has a mother complex. I'm ready and willing to go with him to Spokane or any other place, since he is the only one I have that is not married, but that does not appeal to him. You said you wanted a man with a farm background. Guess he has too much farm background. He is the third generation to live in this delightful little valley, and he has put down his roots so deeply that he cannot be moved, I guess. I do thank you for your interest in him and his ability in writing could be channeled in the right direction. I hate to see it lying dormant, but it is his life.*

...Doug tends to hay fever and a gift for putting words on paper, so he gets lured away from the land a few hours each week, comes home every night to sleep on the land that his grandfather homesteaded in 1870.

Doug in a letter to his mom:

Dear Mom,

No, I am not leaving this note as a farewell as is sometimes done, but more as a clarification of how I feel towards home and my family and which I think will be much easier for a baby, like me, to do than would a tearful heart to heart talk.

The last two or three years, you have been unduly concerned over my always being at home and not having "any fun" etc., thinking that I am bored to death, but on the contrary, I most certainly am not bored, in any sense of the word. I can't think of any place in the world I would rather be than right here and I hope you will never again feel that I'm not happy because I very definitely am.

I'm directing this letter to you mainly because you have been urging me to go to college and to be perfectly truthful, I don't feel like that is what I should do. I dread it, for being away from home. I dread going to Boise for just that one week, because it took me away from home. A home which truly does mean more to me than anything else in the world. I know just as well as I know anything, that I'd never be happy going to school. I've always" bucked off" any conversation concerning it, for that reason I suppose it's like Kathleen but to get what I would want I'd have to take so much trash that I could never use and even if I did go, I'd still never be happy doing anything else except what I'm doing now and I don't need college for that. I, deep down in my heart, enjoy to a certain extent, of different degrees, everything I do here. I'm not dissatisfied with my "lot" and I don't wish I had any more "fun."

The work in the yard this year has been especially invigorating to me and I have enjoyed every minute of it. My turkey venture has been fun and everything else has been fun. Oh yes, I could come home weekends, what's a weekend, when I'm used to the whole week.

I want to be here to help with the production and promotion of "Rugged Rhymes," to continue my associations with the Firth Record, I want to be here to help "get out" the beets, blue spuds and most of all I just want to be here. I have too much on my agenda to leave it for something that I don't really want, when I can be here and do just what I want to do. Can't you see it that way?

Lovingly,   your Doug

(Mimi wrote) Kay has been trying to get Doug to go with him to school in Pocatello. I was all pepped up about it. Thought it would be such a nice thing for those

two to go together. Dad kept saying that he didn't think Doug wanted to go. He liked us too well to leave us. Finally, when he had to decide, he cried and told us that he was perfectly happy with his home and with his family and did not want to go. We all feel better now. I've always been afraid that he was not getting a square deal and should get some more schooling while there is money to be had. I know he wrote to you about it so I know you understand too. Now, I shall be hoping for the green house to cease being a dream house and come true. I said to him, "Dougie, you devote yourself to me so much, what will you do if anything should happen to me?" He said, "Well that will be soon enough to think about it when it does?" So, I shan't worry any more about him being bored and unhappy.

Wallace Richard
May 2, 1929 - Sept 5, 2015

Married Marlene Stibal
Sept 28, 1950

Children

Debbie	Aug 9, 1951	Married Steven Blaser, divorced children, Justin, Shawn Married George Oleson – child, Mimi
Casey William	May 1, 1955	Married Carol Butler, divorced children, Tye, Lucas, Conner
Cindy Lou	March 23, 1959	Married Wayne Telford –children, Dusty, Sammy
Clifford Wallace	July 21, 1962 - Oct 9, 2000	Married Tammy Lee John, divorced child, Cason (mother Tandra Powell)

(James Reid wrote to Nellie) *There is no news here worth mentioning only we have a new baby boy here at the Reid-Just ranch. A big fine fellow with black hair and dark blue eyes named Wallace at my suggestion. You know they have one named Douglass and I said if you are naming your sons after Scottish heroes call him Wallace which they did. And if he makes as brave and loyal a man as the man he is named after he will be all right.*

Wally remembers riding with his dad and being scared as he whipped the horse with the reins and went too fast. Wally always wanted to go to work with his big brothers but as soon as they took him, he would want to go home. They were always nice and let him tag along. He could saddle his own horse so he would come and go as he wanted. Wally said he really appreciated his brother's good treatment. He knew other boys that were treated badly. For instance, Frank in the Alvin Just family was called a 'panty waist,' or a 'smart woman.'

Wally liked to play with good little rubber animals; much better than you can buy now. He would put nails between the wood planks on the living room floor, then wrap string around the 'posts' for his fence. Mimi let him leave up the farm for weeks at a time in the big room.

He remembered getting a bike for Christmas one year. He rode it up and down the kitchen floor and never remembers getting reprimanded.

(Mimi wrote) *Wallace is so much like his father in build. Long arms and legs and no meat on them. My brother Fred used to call Rufus, "Stork," and there is nothing Wallace resembles more.*

When Fred was away in the army, the shots for Grandy's asthma were given by Wally, still a teenager.

Wally did most of the round-up work after Grandy died. He, Jim Mattson, and Neily Stoddard were good friends and they were the young cowboys. Dad said he started going to the round-up later. Wallace bought a van (big white trailer) to sleep in. Dad remembered one day there was 14 inches of new snow, so they stayed in the trailer all day. The cattle all wanted to go to the valley.

Wallace was a teen when his dad died. He felt obligated to stay out of school because he was needed on the farm. He and Doug were the first ones to go to High School. Wallace wanted to play basketball and did, even though he missed sign up. We found the letter to the coach of the basketball team asking him to please let Wally play. The family greatly enjoyed going to the games.

(Mimi wrote in 1946) *When old Squint (Jim Just) heard that Wallace had started to high school he said, "Well that's all right. High school is like church. It won't hurt anybody."*

Wally had been married for a few years. He caught his thumb in 'the dallies' (the rope) while branding. He blamed the rag gloves he was wearing. Dad said the thumb was still attached a little and the doctor tried to save it but it didn't take. It is just the tip of the thumb that was amputated and didn't seem to bother him at all.

Wallace got a 1A draft rating (available for military service), but Mimi worked to get a deferment for him because they needed him at home since Grandy was so sick at the time. We found the card in the old house and I told Marlene. They never heard that he had been accepted. She was hurt that Mimi hadn't told them. She said Wally would have loved to serve his country.

Grandy

This letter was written to Jerrie from Mimi when she was going to marry Eldro. It was printed in the Shelley Pioneer Nov 39, 1906

My dear girl:

When I speak of his father, I wish I could finish by saying "and you will find Big Boy the counter part of his father" but I cannot say it. He has many attributes of my people, some of them may be to his advantage, but many of them I know are not. From the time I first met his father, more than a quarter of a century ago, he has been the most patient, the most serene, and the most comfortable companion that anyone can imagine.

In the few misunderstandings we have had, and they have been very few, I have always been the transgressor, the one that was quick to anger and quick to say cruel things. Somewhere along the shady lane about the house is a tree, a large tree that Daddy told me a short time ago was planted one day when we were first married. I should have been with him but I was offended about some foolish little thing and he planted it by himself, it breaks my heart to think of it. If the tree had only died so that he could have forgotten that I was unkind to him, but by its growing it has been a sad reminder.

Our first meeting was a queer one; in fact we didn't meet paradoxically as that may sound. I had come home for the Christmas vacation from the State Normal school and my father took me immediately to the place where he had a big crew of men working on a prospective power site. It was in the days of open saloon and there was some great joke about a certain young man having been the worse from imbibing too freely the day before. The reason my attention was especially drawn to this young man, I found him very good looking, very tall and very bashful. My brothers were on the work with him but no one introduced us. I can see him yet, there in the December sunshine wearing a heavy gray mackinaw.

After that we met at the Post Office, which was kept by my mother but we were hardly able to find anything to say but the simplest observations about the weather. I went back to school but in June came home with a nervous breakdown and was in bed for weeks. One day when I was better this same tall young man was in the yard and I asked my mother to tell him as he rode away to ride past the window so that I could see him. I did not attach any significance to the strange request and I don't think my mother did. It seemed to me that he meant the out of doors the rhythm of the galloping horse and everything from which I was shut away.

In the fall, the doctor said I was not to go back to school but I could teach a really easy school, anything different. I took a school of eight pupils back in the mountains. I boarded with an aunt of the same tall young man and he was one of my pupils, though more than two years older than I. Perhaps I had not realized what hidden forces were pulling me on to my destiny, but before spring we both realized that I was not going back to school ever, I was just going to stay with this adorable six-footer always.

We were not married for more than a year, however. One of my best friends says to this day that I must have asked Daddy to marry me, he was so bashful. Really, I did not, though I suppose I used woman's prerogative to the limit to assure him that I would say yes.

All through the years I can see him kind to us all, doing his utmost to make us all happy. When Big boy was perhaps about three, I can see him running and crying: "Daddy did not kiss me good-by," then I can see Daddy, just barely within sound of the little voice, leaving his team and coming patiently back to kiss the little tyke and leave him satisfied. Most fathers would not have had time but maybe the time he took then is what makes Big Boy what he is today. Maybe that is partly the reason that Big Boy in spite of his six feet of fine manhood still kisses Daddy good bye. Maybe it is all these little things that have made him worthy of your love.

In later years, there came to us what would seem a great opportunity to most people. Some fine friends, who held high positions and command large salaries wanted to take our Vin and send him to school, take him into their home and treat him as their own, let him be a brother to their boy. All the world said we were foolish nearly all the world, but Daddy said "No," "Why" he said "the reason there are so many crooks in the world is because people are all letting someone else raise their children for them" I did not want to make the decision but I am so glad he decided that way. Another time the stands out in my memory though trivial in itself, Big boy hurt Vin's feelings by some thoughtless remark. Daddy told me about it and my first inquiry was: "Did you tell Big Boy that Vin was hurt?" "No," he said, "I didn't. It wouldn't have helped Vin and it would have hurt Big Boy too." Wasn't that the wisest way? I would have spoken too quickly.

Your father once said to me that he would think I'd resent the fact that the boys all love their father so much, because if there is a difference of opinion, I know that they will line up with him. I said I could never resent it because I knew they were sensible and anyway, it is a complement to me. I chose a good father for them. I hope you will love him just as they do and I believe you will. He is the kind that you must know well to appreciate thoroughly.

May your husband grow more like Daddy with each passing year, is the prayer of his mother.

Grandy was tall and thin like his sons, only more so. He stood 6'3" and probably never weighed more than 175 - 180 pounds.

Ronald Hughes said that my son, Ace, looks the most like him of the next generation. Ronald was shopping one day and around the corner came a little boy. Ronald knew immediately he was related to Grandy.

(Mimi wrote) *My husband believed that there was never anything gained by bawling anyone out and the longer I live, the more I agree with him...Bob used to say that if people tried as hard to get along as they tried not to get along, there'd be no trouble in the world.*

Alvin Just said he wanted to "*raise his kids like Bob Reid does.*" Robert's best friends were Jim Just, Fred Bennett and Henry Williams. He served on the board of directors for the Federal Land Bank at Blackfoot. He was also a school board member and the teachers roomed with them while teaching the kids at Lower Presto (Jim and June Mattson home).

(Gwen wrote) *Robert loved the land, operated the farm and ranch and raised Hereford cattle. His farming was done with horse power and he loved his animals. He was truly a cowboy, and made a magnificent picture astride a favorite horse. Robert was a real gentleman, so handsome. It was my privilege to know him for 10 years, but he was sick for most of those years.*

(Mimi wrote in 1941) *Caroline (one of the twins) saw Daddy (Robert E. Reid) on the way to Firth. She said to him, "I wrote you a letter today. It said, "I love you."*

Mimi called Robert 'Rufus' while alive, but she mostly called him Bob after he died.

(Mimi wrote) The *first year we were married there was the most interesting man with us for several weeks. He was collecting specimens for bird life in Idaho (for the Smithsonian). He caught a pair of each and skinned them so they could be stuffed and mounted. It was the most difficult and exacting work and Grandy had the most fun helping with it.*

One day when Robert and Mimi were first married, they didn't have a bank account and Robert had a $10.00 bill in his pocket. Somehow it disappeared and they were very upset because that was a huge amount of money in those days. Robert went around saying sadly "I lost my $10.00 bill…I lost my $10.00 bill…" One day the wind blew it back by the house and he changed his chant to "I found my $10.00 bill!!…I found my $10.00 bill!!…"

Mimi was talkative and Robert quiet. Their couple friends were Alvin and Dora Just, and Berkley and Florence Larsen.

Mimi

(Gwen wrote) *Very often Mimi would find articles or letters or some printed matter, she wanted to share with the family. At such times it became a family joke for each one in chorus to ask "How long is it?"...Mimi was an avid reader, and a charter member of the Idaho Falls chapter of Idaho Writers League. Agnes was often a guest of programs as a result of her writings...Reading is also greatly enjoyed by the authoress. Her set of Hubbard is her favorite. "We bought it when we could ill afford it and oh, it's been a joy to me!"*

Mimi would want to share something she had read, she would say, "I wish I had written this" or "I would have written that just like he did."

For over 40 years they subscribed to the *Readers Digest*. In the early days she sent for back issues of magazines because they were cheaper. Great bundles of back issues came usually in the spring.

(Deloris Henscheid wrote) *In the 70's while I was teaching at St Margaret's School in Blackfoot, the Franciscan Sisters, interested in local history, read Letters of Long Ago. I made arrangements for the Sisters to meet the author. I loaded the old van with excited nuns, dressed in their black habits and drove out the familiar beloved road. Before long I again sat at the intriguing big table, watching, marveling as Agnes held court for five enthralled students of history.*

Mimi had many friends, fans and acquaintances, and always had people coming and going while we were growing up.

(Mimi wrote of the outfit she planned to wear to the writer's conference) *See you soon. I have a new hat and new shoes but nothing for the in-between section.*

Mimi found good in everyone and was lavish with her praise. She wasn't always as tactful as she wanted to be.

Mimi's Writings

Poetry

She was a frequent author of the Poem of the Week, which appeared in the Post Register. Her poems were about everyday things and people she loved.

(Mimi wrote In April, 1944) *I went to Cora Monson Christensen to read my verses. Cora said, "The thing I like about your poetry, Agnes, is that you have glorified the common-place." I liked that. I hope I have.*

(Mimi wrote) *Mine is not really poetry. It is just thoughts in rhyme.*

In the years, Agnes was busy raising a family she still found time to write. She had two poems published "My Solitude" and "Man in Rubber Boots" in the Denver Post. She was 26 then. Agnes would often take her little typewriter along and write a column or bits of poetry while waiting at the mailbox or appointments. She challenged herself to write a poem every day.

(Mimi wrote) *I hate to have you cry over my verses, but that is the greatest compliment that you could pay me. The first time I began to think maybe I could write, was when Eldro cried over some of my verses. (I think he wasn't more than six but that was the test.)*

(Mimi wrote) *Rhyming ads are sometimes used by the best magazines. I long ago discovered it was easier for me to get in the back door of a magazine than the front door. I sold a rhyming ad to Gillette Razor Company for 20 dollars. I think I might have had more but when they accepted it and asked me to put a price on it, I was so inexperienced I had no idea whether to say one dollar or one thousand. Denton Sleeping Garments Company did not pay me cash but they sent lovely sleepers for my boys that had a decided cash value and the additional satisfaction that goes with feeling that your children are clothed in poetry.*

The Range Cayuse

The Range Cayuse, published in 1916, contained the poetry she had written before the age of thirty. (Mimi wrote) *I have found a place where I could have my Range Cayuse republished in a very inexpensive edition. I have them for fifteen cents.*

Songs of the Soil

Mimi had a book of poems published in 1941 *Songs of the Soil*. Our favorite was the following poem about the pioneers' sacrifices that make our life easier.

Our Gratitude

We're grateful to you, pioneers,
Our hats are off to you,
You've left a mighty heritage
To us the chosen few.

You came with dauntless courage
To till the virgin sod,
To you we sing our praises,
Brave pioneers, and God.

You left your homes and loved ones
To seek this wonder land,
And finding, passed it on to us
Improved on every hand.

You dressed in tattered garments
That we might have the silk,
You drank the water, alkali
That we might have the milk.

You suffered in the wintry blasts
And summer's scorching heat,
That we might live in mansions
And have the best to eat.

You walked through mountain vastness
Through sand and prickly pear
That we might ride in luxury
On rubber, soft, and air.

You tamed the savage races,
You killed the snake and bear,
You plowed the hard, resisting soil
And put the water there.

You've done it all, you pioneers,
There's little left to do.
But all our lives will be a prayer
Of gratitude to you.

Mimi knew firsthand the sacrifices made by the pioneers, and how she and her own children reaped the rewards of the work of the previous generation.

Rugged Rhymes

Grandy suggested the title *Rugged Rhymes* for Mimi's poetry book published in 1948. Agnes felt that using the term "rugged" in the title meant that she was not making any claims of being a polished poet. This book contains her poems written between ages of 30 and 60.

(Mimi wrote) *Some new people moved into the neighborhood and I gave the wife one of my books of verse (Rugged Rhymes). When the husband looked through it, he said; "there are some verses that I carried with me in the mission field, but I did not know they were Mrs. Reid's."*

Autumn Leaves

Autumn Leaves, published in 1965, contained all the poems she wrote after she turned 60.

(Mimi wrote) *"Autumn Leaves," we couldn't believe it was so inexpensive. They did a thousand for $189.00 and they will do the next thousand for two thirds of that figure. They even paid the postage all that long way.*

(Mimi wrote) *People who write poetry do not expect to get rich, so I priced Autumn Leaves at 50 cents. They are so pretty and so easy to read that they are just right for small gifts.*

(Jerrie wrote to Mimi) *A queer thing and a very nice one just happened to me. I was reading the paper (we subscribe to the Boise Capital news) and as usual, turned to Poets Corner or rather, Idaho verse, thinking as I did so, "I don't know why I bother to read this one, the whole is certainly pretty poor stuff." But even as I was thinking that, title caught my eye, "Wild Roses." The tears sprung up and I saw Eldro with a wild rose in his hatband. His yearly tribute to love and beauty and that intangible something that is the spirit of our union. I thought, "I must clip that, for it will mean something to me." Then I read it, and how strange it said the very things that had raced through my mind at the sight of the title. You may find it hard to believe, but I swear it is the truth, that not until I had finished the last words did I see (the author) - Agnes Just Reid, Firth. Wasn't that a lovely thing to happen to me?*

I was not conscious of the fact that your husband brings you wild roses every year, and perhaps you did not know that never once has Eldro failed to bring them to me each summer. No doubt it is copied from his father either knowingly or subconsciously, for he has of course seen his father go through this sweet little ritual. Anyway, I am happy that they both do bring wild roses, and I am glad you wrote a poem about it and that I found it, quite unexpectedly.

(Jerrie wrote to Mimi) *Oh, how I wish you could have seen our beet-raising "Boy" when I read him your poetry this morning. I think you would never, ever, have needed any more reward for anything you have written or may write. The incident has gone down in my history as one of my greatest treasures, one of life's high moments. I didn't look at him until I'd finished and then as I glanced up, I saw that the tears were spilling into his plate. When I went over to him, he put his arms around me and his head on my breast and just sobbed and sobbed and held me tight. He didn't say anything afterward. I don't think he could. It means a lot, when you've broken your back and frozen your toes over a job, to have someone realize all you've done and write of it as powerfully and beautifully as you have done. Oh, I love you for writing it and him for appreciating it.*

I would love to know which poem this was. Mimi wrote often about the trials and triumphs of farming.

Good Reviews and Rejections

(Mimi wrote) *For many years I've kept a Butterfly box so that I can save the nice things that have been said about me. It will warm my heart on the coldest day.*

(Mimi wrote) *I found your review of Letters of Long Ago and wondered if I ever thanked you for it. I doubt if I did. The reason? I was too bashful at that time; I thought editors of all description as something very special. Anyway, your review was beautifully done and it still is and you'll never know how much it meant at that time. I had taken my books to the Cook Drug Company to put them on sale and Mrs. Cook, about the age I am now, gave me the worse trimming I have ever experienced. She assured me without glancing at the lovely Caxton binding, that no one would ever read a book I had written. Hallowell was glad to take them on consignment and could hardly get them in fast enough. But your review took a lot of the sting out of my encounter with Mrs. Cook. Later they came from Texas and New Jersey but yours was the one that saved my life.*

(Mimi wrote about reviews of the Letters of Long Ago.) *They are better than the book itself.*

(Mimi wrote, quoting a judge of one of her stories) *"This is an exceedingly bad story."*

(Mimi wrote) *My husband sort of endured my writing, but after years and years he became quite a fan.*

(Mimi wrote after a rejection from Farm Journal.) *Never had I felt so sure of an acceptance and never was I so low over a rejection.*

(Mimi wrote) *One of my older pieces was used by the LDS Church in one of their lesson manuals. My name was left off.*

Correspondence

(Mimi wrote) *I even have a letter from Pearl Buck written on a machine that needed the type cleaned, but unmistakably her own letter and her own signature. I prize it...*

Before Christmas I got as high as 26 (letters) *in a day...*

One of my best friends (Nelle Vincent) returned a bunch of my letters. Some of them were forty years old and there were things in them, happenings in the family, that I would swear didn't happen. So how can we write history?

Earl Waylon Bowman was a friend of Mimi's. He wrote *The Ramblin Kid*. When he autographed a copy to her, he wrote, "To the Range Cayuse from the Ramblin Kid." I looked up this man on the internet. His daughter archived memorabilia after his death. In the correspondence section, it told of the 80 typewritten letters to his friend and fellow Idaho author, Agnes Just Reid, from the years 1917 through 1926. Doug said Earl Waylon Bowman also wrote poetry under the title of Father Goose.

Mimi often wrote her opinions on controversial issues to Letters to the Editors in local newspapers.

From the county side of the Farm Journal

My more than 30 feet of sons started out on mother's milk and finished off on homemade bread, says Mrs. Agnes Just Reid, Idaho ranch wife. All are over 40 and four of them have wives who make bread superior to any mother ever made. Their children show promise of being quite like them maybe because of homemade bread. (They go on to mention their homemade bread book, a Farm Journal publication.)

(Mimi wrote) *I sold a story for $4 and a letter for $3.*

LIFE magazine Oct 3, 1955

(Gwen wrote) *She wrote many celebrities and heard from them. Most notable was Ann Lindbergh, author of "Gift from the Sea," wife of Charles Lindbergh who was first to solo from U.S. to Europe in his plane, The Spirit of St. Louis. It was like a personal loss to Mimi and Granddad when the Lindbergh's 1st born son was kidnapped and killed.*

Ann Lindbergh had published her book *Gift from the Sea*. Mimi had written to Ann and was picked as one of the women to be featured in Life Magazine. Quoted from Life magazine cover: *Dear Mrs. Lindberg: In the 'Gift from the Sea' women find own isles of Tranquility. It has brought a surprising response from American women who have sat down by the hundreds to start letters with "Dear Mrs. Lindbergh" and tell the author how acutely she has echoed the problems of their lives and how imaginative she has voiced their aspirations. On these pages are pictures of some of the women. With them are excerpts from their letters in which they tell how they have sought, amid the encroaching demands of modern life, their own versions of the tranquility.*

(Mimi wrote) *Ann Lindbergh had expressed the same idea in Gifts from the Sea so I sent her my verses in a fan letter. Next thing I knew I was called by Life Magazine and told to make a lemon pie on a certain day and meet their photographer at the terminal eighteen miles away. We did and it was fun.*

(By Mimi's picture) *Mrs. Agnes Reid, 68, of Blackfoot, Idaho, who is well known locally as a poetess, says she has used her imagination more for cooking than for verse. She writes to Mrs. Lindberg: "You say, 'And when I cannot write a poem, I bake biscuits and feel just as pleased.' Once I put it this way:*

Artistic Urge
Each day I write a poem
To satisfy my soul
About a lovely sunset
Or how the breakers roll.

Today I cannot write one
No matter how I try
And still my soul is satisfied
I've baked a lemon pie.

(Mimi wrote) *The Life photographer came from New York and took more than a hundred pictures of me. It really was the high spot in my life.* The photographer took several other shots that weren't published but given to the family, with the grandkids from Donna up to Barb in the house waiting for a piece of pie.

After the article in *Life* ran, Mimi got a letter from another woman that had been selected, her picture taken, but wasn't included in the publication. They continued a letter correspondence for many years.

(Mable wrote after seeing Mimi and Doug in the *Life* magazine.) *Now I am almost famous just having my aunt's and my cousin's picture in Life. Oh, it is a great Life. And to think it is the first picture and I believe it is the biggest! And it is so good of all of you. The coffee pot, the stove, the dishes, the cousin Doug carrying the wood, everything is good. And such a wonderful picture of the leading lady.*

(Mimi wrote a letter to Montgomery Ward) I *think you owe me a winter wardrobe and I think you will to, if you look at the Life magazine for Oct 3rd. On page 118 is a picture of me taken in a* Montgomery Ward *dress. I ordered the dress in July or August, I was photographed the 29th of August and the magazine was in our mail box the 29th of September, fast work for Life and good advertising for you.*

Columns

Mimi had a column for 40 years. They were under the title of "*Looking at the World*" and later "*Here's a Thought*".

(Mimi wrote in a letter to Ursella Bennett, Jack's wife) ....*I think you know I write a weekly column for the local paper and I can see that it is going to be very good for giving me ideas when my mind seems empty. I don't get paid for the work but I think it is good for me, even if no one else ever reads it. It keeps me from getting kitchen minded and keeps me from thinking of the asthma for a half hour each week.*

Mimi wrote a tribute in her column to Lyndon B Johnson. Here was his reply: "*Dear Mrs. Reid: It was so kind of you to send me that most understanding column and I want you to know how much I appreciate the warmth and generosity of your words.*" He signed it himself.

(Mimi wrote) *All my life I have believed in obituaries for the living. I think I do that kind of thing better than anything else and the pay matters so little to me. I care so little for the things that money will buy.*

(Mimi wrote) *The columns that I think are best never get a comment, but if I wrote a bad one, many seem to like it. Perhaps I should add that I have never been paid for my column. I even pay the postage, but I have nailed down a great many ideas that would otherwise have gone floating away.*

"It's good for a person to sit down and have a deadline" says Mrs. Reid "especially now when people might think I'm getting old."

Letters of Long Ago

(Mimi wrote) *It always seems to me that I do my best writing when my mother is the heroine, but it may be just my imagination.*

(From an article quoting Mimi) *A publisher friend in Boise, (Earl Waylon Bowman, the Ramblin Kid) on learning of our mother's experiences hammered at me to write this book. It is literature and you've got to get it down while your mother is here.*

(Mimi wrote) *I have a letter from a daughter of Thomas Moran, the artist. I had sent him a copy of my* Letters of Long Ago. *The daughter wrote that he was too ill to read it but she had read it to him and he remembered the incident of seeing my mother mold butter in a little cellar in Idaho.*

The first publication of *Letters of Long Ago* was in 1923. Emma lived all the events portrayed in the book but Mimi wrote them in letter form to George Thompson, Emma's father living in England. Emma wrote such letters to her father, but they didn't survive the years. Emma read everything off the typewriter to assure correctness. The book was printed 3 weeks after Emma died; that was a disappointment to Mimi, that her mother never got to hold the book. It took 3 or 4 years to write it. Emma was sick and Mimi was raising a family. I was surprised that in those years Emma was writing a daily diary and never mentioned the book they were working on.

When Kenny and Emma Jean Cosgrove died, the Clarks (my family) were willed the contents of their home. We found an old book *Riding the High Country* by Tucker and Coats. It had been published by the Caxton Publishing company like *Letters of Long Ago*. On the dust cover other books are mentioned. It reads Reid, Agnes Just <u>Letters of Long Ago</u>, Illustrated. 118 pages, 8 vow, Bound in art boards $1.25.

(Mimi wrote about *Letters of Long Ago*) *Be careful about loaning it. There are some LDS people who resent it and have in a few cases torn out the pages that refer to the Morrisite trouble. One of my very best LDS friends told another friend that I should never have put that chapter in it. It would not be the story of my mother's life without those dramatic incidents, things that do not happen to many people. A good friend at Montpelier loaned her copy to a friend and when she tried to get it back, the friend declared she never had it, so my friend felt sure it was burned. They were both good LDS women but they just did not see eye to eye on "Letters of Long Ago." Had I ever dreamed that anyone would resent the story, I'd have never written it, but I had heard my mother tell that story to Mormon, Jew and Gentile and they all knew it was the truth but showed no antagonism then.*

…When the book was published, the niece who did the drawings was in school at Logan and many told her it was a pack of lies. It was a terrible shock to me. So, at the Idaho Falls public library, the book is not loaned any more. Too many copies have been lost or the pages torn out, so keep it if you wish, but be careful about letting it fall into the hands of narrow-minded Mormons.

(Mimi wrote) *I am having a second edition of "Letters of Long Ago." Caxton's are bearing half the expenses of course I cannot dictate this time. They are making the new edition very different. They will not seem at all like themselves but maybe we'll get used to them in time. Anyway, they will be much more durable.*

When Mimi was 86 the University of Utah wanted to put *Letters of Long Ago* back in publication. They wanted the family's consent and were pleasantly surprised that Mimi was very much alive and thrilled to give her permission. She was interviewed and additional history was added to the introduction. The university researched every detail and found only one mistake, by one year. They supplied a complete foot note section and index in the back. Only Mabel's ink pictures were eliminated in the 3rd printing. The edition included many photos.

(Mimi wrote) *The University of Utah has taken over the publication of Letters of Long Ago. It will be a deluxe edition that sells for 6 dollars. I had put out the two editions a thousand copies each, at my own expense, now the bills are all paid by the University.*

(Mimi wrote about errors) *So many escaped us (Doug and herself) in both my books. My mother died while "Letters of Long Ago" was on the press. My husband died while "Rugged Rhymes" was on the press so we read both proofs though blinded with tears. It still grieves Doug that they got past us but I've learned to not care. Doug wished they had sent a copy for him to proof read. (*They were all sad that Vin was misrepresented as "Ben".) *My eyes focus on such a small area now that I seem to see errors better than I ever did, but that is about all they are better for. My distance sight is not good. Cannot tell my boys apart down by the corral gate. It doesn't matter, though I love them just the same.*

A year after Milon died, Mabel was going through her things and found a manuscript by Mimi. Written in the same letter form as *Letters of Long Ago*, only this time, it was to Cousin Lucy in England. It told Emma's life from the time the Thompson family left England as Mormon converts. You can tell that most of the letters are from Emma's journal. What a find! It was printed with help of the Presto Preservation Association and entitled *Letters of Longer Ago*.

Mimi's Philosophy

Character

Drinking was forbidden and talked about very often. Mimi was terribly disgusted with drunks. Grandy did have a beer once in a while. He had chewing tobacco in the barn. He never chewed or drank around Mimi. He or the boys didn't cuss around her. Vin said "there was good cussers and bad cussers."

Democrat

(Mimi wrote) *I have been a violent Democrat since I was eleven.*

Mimi's favorite presidents were John F Kennedy and Franklin Roosevelt. She once attended a lecture by Eleanor Roosevelt.

(Mimi wrote) *President Franklin Roosevelt told his son there were three things for a speaker to remember in making a speech: "be sincere, be brief and be seated."...Cousin Ethel assured us that there'd never be another election. The Roosevelts had taken over. The Democrats would reign supreme forever.*

Mimi and Doug were very sad when President Roosevelt died. She was in Portland with Grandy. Doug made a valedictorian speech about him for his graduation. Since Mimi was away, he wrote his speech by himself and was very proud of it. Doug was in a play at the time and putting out the *Firth Register* paper.

Agnes ran for State Senate in the 1960's. Doug was the campaign manager.

(Mimi wrote) *I think this is the smartest thing I did in the campaign. I knew that my age would be used against me. So, I put an ad in the papers that read something like this "I'm 13 years younger than David O. McKay and I'm thirty years wiser that Bill Burgeson." The nicest thing about that is that the young, the handsome Bill Burgeson rushed up to Carl Hayden, Doug's boss, and asked Carl what he could do about it. Carl simply said: "There's nothing you can do about it. It is a fact."*

(Mimi wrote after losing the election.) *I just keep thinking how wonderful it is that nearly 4000 people cast their votes for me and they were all my friends. That is, I had no backing of church, or lodge, or grange or POE Sisters, All the votes were what my friends rustled for me.*

...running for the Senate I went into this positional game thinking that it would be fun. I'd make some new friends and have some interesting activities. I did, but never did it enter my mind that I could lose friends by it. I have. I've lost friends that I have esteemed for forty years...I dropped out of the race for there were three strikes against me. I was too old, I was a woman and I had no church affiliation.

Women's Rights and Marriage

(Mimi wrote) *A woman should stay in the home from the time the first child is born until the youngest one is of age...the boy who had a different gal every night finds it hard to be satisfied with just one girl, even after he has heard "until death do us part"...People, married people and single people should know there are great many worthwhile things besides sex. But the idea that sex is the most important thing in life is ruining more homes, driving more people into mental unbalance than any other one thing.*

(Mimi wrote) *It seems to me that since women got the right to vote, they have crowded more and more into the affairs of men. Until it is almost like the story of the Arabian and his camel. They have almost slipped all the nose in the tent. The story is that "God created them, male and female." If God had wanted them to be all male, why didn't he make them all male? Women are so unreasonable in their demands. They feel perfectly competent to fill a position in man's domain, but they still expect to be given a seat where they are scarce, while the men stand. I have five sons, I think they are just average in intelligence and I think I'm also average in intelligence, but I was forced to admit, by the time each son was about thirteen, he knew a great deal more on most subjects than I did. It was meant to be that way.*

...I'm in favor of sending woman back home. We need good wives and mothers more than we need more college graduates. I'd suggest that we just work a little harder on bringing up children that are not delinquents.

Against Guns and War

(Mimi wrote) *I've written rhymes and won stuff, even won a Beebe gun once and quickie threw it into the river to end all wars. What a laugh.*

Spirituality

Mimi and Grandy weren't religious, but had a strong belief in living each day the best they could and showed by practice a deep love for neighbors and family.

The boys didn't have much religious training. They read the Bible in school each morning. There was a time that Mimi almost joined the Mormon Church. The day she was to join, for some reason Robert asked her to help him do something. He said "you can join another day, can't you?" She agreed that she could, but never got around to it.

(Mimi wrote) *March 7, 1943 Gwen had been up and she and I were talking about Sunday, church, etc. She said Sunday just felt different to her than any other day. As we went to bed, I was telling Dad about it. He said, "Sunday feels different to me too. It seems like God's day. God and I kind of talk things over on Sunday."*

The Young Reid Boys in the Old House

Seems everyone had a nickname in the Reid family. Agnes's mother, Emma Just, was Gaggy. She lived with the Reid family but died when my dad was small. Grandy's dad, James, was called Gam. Gam was there for most meals and lived long enough for all the boys to know him. Wally was 7 when he died. They both loved the grandkids and they loved them back.

The boys got to wear long pants when they were about 2 years old. The custom of wearing dresses until that time was for the ease of changing diapers. Dad said they mostly wore overalls as kids.

The Reid family was like two families, the older three boys, then a space of eight years before the younger two, Doug and Wallace.

Fred, Doug and Wally remember having terrific leg cramps and their dad walking them around during the night.

Doug and Wally remember fighting by the iron fence and Mimi saying to them, "if you want to fight, I will give you a fight," and as she was coming, she picked up a switch. They ran and she didn't hit them.

Dad remembers being swatted with the fly swatter by Mimi. He couldn't remember what he did wrong. That was the only time he recalled being disciplined.

(Mimi wrote) *I never did want to be rich.*

The windmill was operable since Agnes was 18. I think as long as the wind blew it kept the tank full. They could also pump it as Fred did when they were fighting the attic fire. The Reids had lots of butter, cream, cottage cheese, eggs, beef, lamb, chickens and pork, all raised on the farm. Grandy smoked all the hams and bacon.

The outhouse was in back of the iron fence. The bathroom was put in the old house in 1951 in the space that lead to the stairs going down in to the cellar.

The attic was used for sleeping for the boys and hired men. We know the boys also slept with their folks in the big room. There was a stairway outside of the house so you could enter and exit the attic without going through the house.

The Reids had telephones before Dad was born or at least before he could remember. He said it was mounted on the wall and you spoke into the front mouth piece and held an ear piece that was attached to it with a cord. Their number was R3, Larsen's R2, Jim Just R1, and the Bennett's was J3. An operator in Blackfoot would connect every call. Dad remembers that the Hayes home was 63 and the store was 70.

The Reids got a radio when Dad was about 15. Their favorite radio program was *Lem and Abner*. It was about two store owners and other characters that would come in to visit. The first radio was a car radio that was hooked up to work in the house. A wire strung to the white house where Jerrie and El were living provided them with a radio too, but they had to listen to the same program that was on at the main house.

About every day someone would go up to check the gauge in the river. I assume it was a stationary pole that would measure how high the flow of water was. They couldn't do anything to change it but maybe they kept a record for someone who could.

The kids all rode horses to school. It was about 3 miles to the Lower Presto School (later the Jim and June Mattson home). Dad and his older brothers stopped going to school after the eighth grade, but Doug and Wallace graduated from Firth High school. They would drive vehicles to high school.

Mimi was sentimental and you could find her crying at any time of the day over something she read. Grandy would get teary too, a trait the boys inherited.

Fred spent a lot of time as a kid, sitting on the water reservoir on the old stove, (to warm water) talking with his brothers. This continued after they were married.

(Mimi wrote in a letter to Kittie) *We are all feeling rich and prosperous and contented. No special reason for it, except that we had a good holiday yesterday and rested it off to the music of another million-dollar rain. We had not shut up the calves so there was no milking, the irrigating was going merrily on, I had filled the wood box, the coal bucket and the potato basket while waiting for the men to come to supper the night before. So in place of Rufus getting up at four as he has been doing, we all got up between eight and nine. Now I have a fire in the fire place and can tell you all about it.*

(Mimi wrote) *One of the funny things that we have kept going through the years is the story about the new hired man when the boys were still small. It was springtime and at that time of year the sun would just be setting just as we came to the evening meal. My husband remarked about the sunset and everyone at the far end of the eight-foot table jumped up to get a better view. Only the new man was left ladling gravy over his potatoes. After we had all had the "pause that refreshes" we returned to our places and the new man looked up from under his shaggy pale red eyebrows and said with astonishment: "Is zat the first time the sun ever set out here?"*

Play

The boys played marbles, shooting other people's and winning them. Wally said marbles were still the rage while he was in Firth High School. He was in awe of the skill of two fellows. They would squat and shoot and never miss a marble at 6 ft. My grandma Daphne as a child would dig out the natural occurring clay balls from a bank in Orderville and called them "Doughbies." Dad called them "clay babies." They were for sale but the Reid's bought the glass ones. He said they would use a glass one as their shooter marble as they were perfectly round and accurate. He had some natural marbles but they were some he won.

Doug remembers throwing a striped marble at Fred's head through an open car window.

The Fourth of July was celebrated with presents of pop-guns. One time they went to Idaho Falls to watch a "battle" where people would shoot Roman candles at each other.

Car tires were narrower and taller when Dad was a boy. He and Vin would spend hours rolling them around "being" cars, or "driving" cars, he didn't know which. They each had their own tires. Vin called his 'the cream colored Suttee,' which was a luxury vehicle at the time. Sometimes marbles were cattle in their play.

When they were playing horse, they would break off a branch and stick it between their legs. They could swish it back and forth like a tail. Dad remembered that Norma Reid would whinny when they played horse.

Vin remembers a $5.00 used pool table when he was young. It was in the middle of the living room. They all played, but Vin was the pool shark. Doug threw a billiard ball and broke the light switch by the living room door by the hall. This pool table is still in Vin's basement.

The first "talky" movie Dad ever saw was "The Virginian." He said he especially liked the cows making realistic sounds.

(Mimi wrote) *TV is not so popular since the weather is good, but gingerbread is.* The Reids would play a game, "You have a face." One would start, you have an "Angry face," the next would say "You have a Beautiful face," and on down the alphabet.

Birthdays were celebrated with a layer cake and a present. Dad remembers "pinto" cakes. Some of the batter was white and put in the pan. The rest of the batter was colored with cocoa then added in dollops to the pan. A knife was used to barely mix, resulting in a marbled look.

Dad said they had electric lights for their Christmas tree run by the generator. He remembers candles on the tree, but after they were lit they were watched carefully until they were blown out.

Their Christmas stockings were hung on the fireplace, just regular stockings from their drawers. They got presents from their parents and Santa but he doesn't remember giving presents to each other.

(Mimi wrote) *Maybe I am not so old as I thought I was, for I enjoyed it more than I have a circus in years. One thing, it was the coolest, lovely day. Another thing, it is the only place my husband will ever go without protest. I've been going to circuses with him for many years and I always enjoy it.*

The Reid family went to the American Falls Dam dedication and had 3 flat tires on the car getting there. That was in the old days when the tire was taken off, patched and put back on.

(Mimi wrote) *Buck (Kittie Reid Bower's son) is here, he is Fred's particular friend.* Grandy used to say: Baked apples she sold, and cranberry pies, and this is the lady, who never told lies

Mimi and Grandy, with El and Vin, went to the World's Fair in San Francisco in 1916. This picture was taken on their trip. The photographer would send the print to people soon after it was taken. That rivals smart phones today.

Grandy, with Vin on his lap, is seated next to Mimi right above the man standing on the ground. El is barely visible beside Grandy.

When the neighborhood kids would come to spend the evening with the boys, Grandy and Mimi would join in the fun.

Dad remembers coloring Easter eggs with capsules of dye.

Mimi and Bob slept many summer nights in a big, (at least 10 by 10) green tent. It had a floor and a bed in it. Wally said he though he had something to do with the horse Banjo, kicking a hole in the side of the tent.

(Mimi wrote) *May 25, 1940. Vin took the car at 9:30, after a hard day's work, and took Wallace away up in Cannon's field to get some birch stick-horses. What a brother? What patience! What kindness!*

Airplanes were fun to see when Dad was growing up. When they heard one, they would run outside and watch it until it disappeared. After he got back from being in the army, he heard a plane and ran outside to watch it. Doug informed him they didn't do that anymore.

Music

(Mimi wrote) *Doug can carry tunes. This morning he woke up singing "*Home Sweet Home.*" Says he likes that record because it is so quiet.*

Grandy played the fiddle a little, but the harmonica well. (Debbie Reid Oleson has Grandy's fiddle, handed down from her dad.) Dad remembers buying him a harmonica. "Dry and Dusty" was a favorite song. Doug can't remember him playing the harmonica, so his asthma must have put a stop to it in his later years.

Mimi played the organ and they had some fun singing times. Mimi and Bob sang with Berkley and Florence Larsen at the Goshen church.

Whenever there was a family gathering, Grandy would be coaxed to sing "The Gol' Darned Wheel." Gwen said she was glad she got to hear him sing it.

Doug sang with a choir when he was young.

(Mimi wrote) *12-year-old Doug once sang the song "Daffodils" at a competition. I was right up front so that when someone came to ask you (the Judge) if there were any "finds," you said, "just one outstanding voice. A little boy from Lower Presto." It took me quite a while to realize that, that boy was mine. Becky Hayes had been telling us his voice was something to boast about. He was undersized and shy but he did a good job in that big building and was given the top rating.* (The only soloist chosen at the district music festival held at Shelley.) *A few years later when his voice changed to a man's voice, it never had that special quality again. After nearly thirty years, I wonder why we didn't at least talk to you about him. We didn't even have a record of that voice.*

Doug took a class in school to learn the saxophone. Vin took lessons for saxophone in town. Wally took the trumpet in school. None kept up with their instruments. Fred said all the boys played the phonograph well.

(Mimi wrote) *My husband was the one with the voice, we were the singingest family in the world. And this is the tragic part of it. We never got a recording of it so people will always think it was my imagination. They were making records, but asthma hit before we ever felt rich enough to have it done. He not only had the voice; he had the gift of imitation.*

Mimi had written in a diary about going to the Larsen's and making a record of Grandy and Doug singing. Naida (Berkley and Florence's daughter) had this to say about that day: "I just called mom and she recalls the 45 rpm record and says it was in the old Crosby radio the folks had and she doesn't know what happened to it. She recalls hearing it but is unsure if it was Vin she heard singing the 'Gol Darned Wheel,' and she remembers Alma saying, 'I've got to get my guitar and help him out, he's off pitch.' She doesn't recall Doug but does recall hearing Rufus sing. This may be many memories that jumble up together."

Mimi said that her husband didn't say words of love so much as sing them. They had many favorites together. *(Mimi wrote) For our anniversary, he (Robert) always sang, "Believe me if all those Endearing Young Charms."* I found this beautiful Irish song on the web. Here are some of the lyrics so you can imagine Grandy singing them to Mimi.

> Believe me, if all those endearing young charms,
> Which I gaze on so fondly to-day,
> Were to change by to-morrow, and fleet in my arms,
> Like fairy-gifts, fading away!
> Thou wouldst still be adored as this moment thou art,
> Let thy loveliness fade as it will;
> And, around the dear ruin, each wish of my heart
> Would entwine itself verdantly still!

Work

(Gwen wrote) *Nels was often away from home with his irrigation projects, so Robert, who loved the land, operated the farm and ranch and raised Hereford cattle. His farming was done with horse power and he loved his animals. He was truly a cowboy, and made a magnificent picture astride a favorite horse. Robert was a real gentleman, so handsome. It was my privilege to know him for 10 years, but he was sick for most of those years.*

Jim Just, Bob Reid, and Berkley Larsen ran their cattle together. The bulls were in with the cows year-round. Ranchers now only leave them with the herd for a few months to get the cows bred, which means they have a regular once-a-year calving season.

Mimi would help milk cows and fixed breakfast of usually ham or bacon and eggs.

She made beautiful butter like Emma from a barrel churn that sat sideways. The cream was turned with a wooden paddle.

Ice would be harvested from the Blackfoot River in winter. It would be stored in the cellar. An ice box kept things cold into the summer. Sometimes they made ice cream for a summer treat.

Dad remembers a couple of cattle drives to the stockyards in Blackfoot when he was small. At that time the stockyards sat where the fairgrounds are now. The cattle buyer came out to the ranch ahead of time to make the deal. On the first day they would take them as far as a field owned or leased by Jim Just and Pugmire, near where Gary Pratt lives now. The next day they would go to the yards where they would be loaded on train cars. Dad didn't remember the loading out but said they had to ride all the way home from Blackfoot starting about 3:00 pm.

Each Reid son received a heifer calf when they were 10 years old, and were supposed to receive the money from the sale of calves descended from this cow. Often they were like the rest of us ranchers and the calves had to be sold and the money kept by the parents for running the ranch.

The haying took lots of horse and man work, like every other job on the ranch.

Robert had a huge stack of kindling he readied for winter. Each night before bed he whittled enough shavings to start the morning fire.

The walls and ceilings of their home would be calcimined every so often. This was a form of whitewash, an inexpensive white paint made from calcium carbonate, glue and water used to coat plaster surfaces.

Bob would go about his work whistling and singing like his sons did. A neighbor, Chris Peterson, nicknamed Bob "Whistling Rufus" from a popular song. It was usually shortened to Rufus.

The kids's chores growing up included milking cows. They had 6 -8 cows. They were milked in the morning after the calves had been taken away for the night. The calves would be turned back in after the milking to spend the day with their mothers. They were mostly Jersey, crossbred with a Durham (Shorthorn) Bull. Dad remembers the names of Spike, Cheney, Shorty, Black Jersey, Yellow Jersey.

The milk was brought to the house and poured in the separator to collect the cream from the milk. The milk not used by the family would be fed to the pigs. The thick cream was used by the family or to make butter to sell. They sold cream to the "Cream Station" in Shelley for 10 - 15 years.

Dad remembers Grandy and Mimi going to their friends in Sunnydale that had a Jersey dairy. They took out the back seat of the car, laid down a tarp and brought two baby calves home.

They farmed all the lower fields below the road from Casey's place to where Alvin lived at Ted's place. The existing road was lower than the road is today. The crops were hay, oats and wheat. Later they had smaller fields of sugar beets and potatoes.

They spent all summer haying. When they were hot and sweaty, the boys would shed their clothes by the ditch bank, run across the pasture to the river buck naked, swim down around the bend and then run back to their clothes.

Robert would spend about three hours in the morning, three hours in the afternoon, and three hours in the evening flood irrigating. Ditches sometimes blew out and they would have to get the scraper hitched up to a team and make a new dike.

The Lower Field was put into many different crops before it was let go to pasture. Mom remembers picking potatoes on part of it.

(Mimi wrote) *It is all the things that come to country dwellers free. All the hardships yes, but all the joys too. The joy of finding the first mushroom, the first bluebird, the joy of helping a husband mix grass seed and feeling the different varieties slip through the fingers like particles of gold, the joy of sitting in the barn by the side of a sick calf.*

...At the most important period in the lives of spud raisers, they saw fit to send an extra head of water down the Blackfoot River and took out our private dam. Our boys are raising 150 acres of spuds that must have water every eighth day. It cost them $64.00 an hour to get the dam repaired. It took several days to do it so the spud check will have a terrible dent in it. I'll have to go without that fur coat again this year.

...My husband was the best stacker for miles around and therefore received $1.75 per day when ordinary men just worked for $1.50. Skilled and unskilled you know. If the stacks he built were placed end to end on top of each other they would reach to the stars. I used to sometimes ride a horse out to the fields to see him. To see his work, but

he never came down off the stack till quitting time, kind of long distance "necking." The beautiful handmade stacks that were a work of art. We see no more. They were broad shouldered and solid and so smooth that they looked like a man just leaving the barber shop. Just one of the many changes that seventy years of living brings to you.

The Just side of the family were businessmen. The Reid side liked being farmers and ranchers and, according to Dad, wanted to "continue doing what they were doing."

(Gwen wrote) *Mimi was a very good cook and made us feel welcome. Most always she had a snack waiting for the teachers after school. A great favorite of mine was buttermilk and cookies, especially whole wheat cookies. It was amazing to me how Mimi would take a pan, go from cupboards to the flour box, add ingredients and stir. She used no recipe, except the one in her head and soon a cake, cookies or gingerbread would appear from the oven of the big black oversized wood burning range.*

Mimi made soap from rendered beef fat. This soap would only be used for the laundry.

(Mimi wrote) *Today I have baked eight loaves of bread in the old range. I put in two sticks of wood and went to lie down. In just 45 minutes I got up and every loaf was as evenly brown as if I had painted them. Stoves and women just begin to get good when they are over seventy.*

...I have fried enough eggs for family and hired hands to reach half way around the world. I've heated water in kettles outdoors and washed for a family of ten often including clothes from unmarried helpers. I have worked in the beet field a little, to encourage the boys to like it. I have turned an old-fashioned churn or ice cream freezer with my right hand, held a book or magazine in my left hand and nursed a baby all at one time.

...All good things seem to have granted us. We are awfully hard up, the cattle brought half what they should have, the beets brought almost nothing. Our sugar company could not pay. The whole crop of potatoes brought $80.00 etc, etc. But we are well and we are happy.

Robert, Fred and Vin had a job checking the power line for a few years after it was erected. Vin or Dad would start walking the line, and Bob would drive the other one up a mile and that boy would start walking. As soon as the other would catch up to the car, Bob would pull up another mile and they would leap frog along until they were done. These lines were checked every month, all year. They never found a problem. Chick had a job riding on the reservation doing the same thing.

(Mimi wrote) *Since sometime in October I have made thirteen shirts, seven dresses, two coats and last but by no means least, turned Rufus's overcoat. Every flap and tab and button hole. It was a big job but he has a new overcoat that he could never have had otherwise.* (Mimi worried Robert may be embarrassed to wear it) *I needn't have been. He is very proud of it. The first time he was in town he went into the store where it had been bought and showed it to the manager. It was my turn to be embarrassed. But it was also my turn to be gratified to the soles of my feet. No pay check could have ever equaled that satisfaction.*

One time, Grandy and Eldro were fixing fence somewhere in the Lower Field. A family they didn't know was picnicking in the grove. The kids were playing in a place where the water from the river had made a little pond. A little girl had strayed and made it to the river. Luckily and unbelievably, Grandy was right there to save her from swift water. The story was written up in the Shelley Pioneer and was published in the Grandy edition of the *Presto Press*.

Reid Saves Shelley Girl from River Sunday

Billy Kunter, 7, daughter of Mr. and Mrs. William Kunter of Shelley was saved Sunday by the chance presence of R. E. Reid. Mr. Reid, planning to mend a fence on his field, reached the river just as the child stepped into a sinkhole on the river bank. The Kunters, with a group of Shelley people, had gone to the Reid Ranch at Presto for a picnic Sunday, the first warm Sunday of the year. A group of eight children had gone wading in the river when little Billy stepped off the bank into deep water. There were no adults about except Mr. Reid, who appeared on the scene at the opportune moment. He plunged in after the child as he saw her going down. The current is swift at that place and a moment's delay would have been disastrous.

Family and Love

(Mimi wrote) *If you can give your children but one thing, let it be enthusiasm...When I was first married, I was never jealous of another woman, but I was often jealous of the hired man...The unpleasant incidents in all those years, I could count on the fingers of one hand, the pleasant incidents would fill a book...My husband watched each one of his five sons draw his first breath then he loved them as tenderly as any mother could. He even wished he could give milk so he could feel as necessary as I did.*

...In forty years that I lived with one man, I cannot ever recall a birthday present he bought me. I always carried a check book and when there was money in the bank, we spent it without any special restriction for the things we needed most. I wonder if my emotions were crippled by such an agreement. Anyway, I only had one birthday each year. It was a small portion of the days we spent together, but I do recall that in all those forty years, he was never unkind. We both did everything we could to do something special for the birthdays of the children. I believe as you say that children take things literally but wives are grown up or supposed to be. Another element entered this matter of gifts, a thing you touched upon in your article. If we had chosen a gift that was not exactly appreciated as so often happens in the matter of gifts, it would have been

necessary to pretend we were pleased. Pretense never entered our marriage. I think I bought my husband two or three expensive watch chains. He did not rave that they were just what he needed. He just went on wearing a little piece of leather on his watch so that it did not show and yet was enough to take hold of. I finally accepted the fact that he knew what he wanted to wear on his watch. There were no hurt feelings just better understanding. We never cramped each other's style. We never drove each other crazy and I believe the neighbors would tell you our marriage was a success.

...Maybe we are a freak family, so it is unfair to judge by ourselves but we are the folks I know the best. We have been married thirty years and have seldom been separated for more than two or three days at a time. We never get on each other's nerves. On those rare occasions when we have been apart, we have both been rather miserable. To be in another part of the house, his unfailing question when he opens the door is, "where's mama?" The children, growing up in the atmosphere, have the same devotion of each other. They love to be together. When one is away for a few days the others are positively lost. They feel the need of each other and can visit endlessly over small details of the farm or the neighborhood and always enjoy each other. This is, although the two oldest are married and in homes of their own. My advice to married people would be, "Work together, play together, keep together as much as possible and ensure that 'oneness' that is so necessary to married happiness.

...Perhaps we did not love our children enough but we surely loved them an awful lot and told them so. The neighbors say we raised a wonderful family. Some folks thought it was strange when the five sons grew to be six feet tall that they still kissed their daddy. They seemed to love doing it and I don't think they can be called sissies, even by their enemies, if they have any.

When baby Barbara toddled by Robert, he snatched her up and said *"Come sit on Grandy's lap, little Peaches."*

(Mimi wrote) *The training mind that I like best to think about, is the forty years that my husband and I worked side by side like a well-trained team. Neither one was ever balky, neither one ever tried to shirk on the other, each appreciated the unfailing help of the other. We were not well paid for our labors, but we felt akin to God for we were doing a creative work. Giving a hungry world food and we gloried in it every step of the way. Perhaps my mind is not well trained, but my heart would like to go back to the beginning and do it all over again.*

...Marriage makes a diffusion of personalities. I sometimes suspect I am more Reid than Just.

Mimi and Grandy in their Later Years

These photos taken the same day

Doug, Wallace, Vin, Eldro, Fred (not long before Grandy died)

Mimi had cataract surgery before they could put the lens right in your eye. For the rest of her life, she had to wear thick glasses. Dad said she never looked like Mimi after that.

Bob's brothers Dick, Don, and Bill, also suffered with asthma. I have never heard that Jim, the oldest brother, had symptoms. Kittie never had it as far as I saw, and none of the second generation. I wonder now if modern medicine would have cured Grandy.

He died from complications of asthma at the age of 63 in 1947. He was about 128 lbs. at his death, for a 6'3 frame he had lost a lot of weight in the 9 years of being sick. Mimi thought it had something to do with the house fire since his symptoms started soon after. Mimi would live another 29 years.

(Gwen wrote) *It wasn't long after I came into the family that Robert found he had asthma, bad. It was a most difficult time for everyone. It was so hard to see him fight for breath, even with his 'wheeser' (inhaler). Most of the time he slept sitting up in bed. We waited in vain for a miracle cure, but it wasn't to be.*

Alma never knew him when he wasn't sick. He smoked when he was younger as did all his brothers, so the asthma might be attributed to that. When breathing became too terribly difficult, Fred would be called, day or night, to give him a shot. This went on for years. When Fred was drafted, Wallace took over this job.

Trips were taken in hopes of finding a climate that would help. In 1940 Dad drove Robert, Mimi, Wally and Doug to California to Mabel (Bennett) and Milon Hutchinson's home to see if the climate was agreeable. They spent a month there, then on to Arizona to visit Don and Dick in the Sanatorium. The winter of 1944 – 1945 Robert went to Oregon to try a doctor's treatments. He lived with his brother Don and his wife, Dell, but didn't get any better.

Grandy was in the hospital in Pocatello. The family was staying with Ray and Virginia Brown, Gwen's sister. Dad had spent the night with Grandy, Vin traded him off, and Grandy died soon after.

(Mimi wrote in a letter to Ursella after Grandy died.) *Maybe there are things you'd like to know about Dad. He had not been especially worse. Was only in the hospital three days, but nine years is a long time to be sick and he was just too worn out to rally another time. We don't have any regrets. We did all we could and we are so thankful that he did not go seven years ago in California. The boys who were very small then, are men now, so they are more able to get along without a daddy, but it is hard for any of us to get along without such a daddy as he was.*

Mom (Alma) had this powerful experience. She was walking above the road soon after Robert died. She felt his presence and was assured things would be ok.

(Mimi wrote after Grandy died) *We are going along about as usual. It has been a wonderful fall and the boys have Vin's beets all out, sixteen acres, and are on the last lap of ours, eighteen acres. It has been a long job but they won't have to pay out any to Mexicans. They did the thinning for us too. Wallace does the trucking. He ought to be in school but he thinks no one but him can run Dad's old truck and he may be right. Anyway, he's a dandy little worker. They all are. Doug is the champion topper. Even when Chick is in the crew.*

(Mimi wrote about being 80) *If you have almost eighty years as happy as my life has been there will be no reason for regrets. It has been a great life. I'd like to live another eighty.*

Wallace had an attorney prepare an agreement that Mimi signed before she died that Eldro had been paid off.

(Gwen wrote) In 1976 the family learned Mimi had breast cancer. I say the family learned. Mimi had known for at least 6 years, but kept it to herself for as she explained, there was always an upcoming grandchild wedding, or a new baby due and she just didn't want to spoil the good things or worry anyone with bad news of her own. So, she did nothing. Now it was too late for medical help but being Mimi she made the most of her time left. She was in the Blackfoot hospital about 3 weeks and died just a month before her 90th birthday.

Iris Just (neighbor and friend, wife of Mimi's nephew Chick) wrote about Mimi after she died

My heart is heavy today with the loss of an advisor, a confidant and a truly good friend in the passing of Agnes Just Reid.

I can't remember a time in my life when she wasn't involved in some way. I went to school with her older boys, and was privileged to teach one of the younger boys during my first teaching assignment in the little school at lower Presto.

I remember the fun parties we had at the Reid home when we were teenagers with Bob and Agnes entering the games with all the rest of us. The big table in the long kitchen was always overflowing with tasty food to satisfy young appetites.

After my marriage into the family, I lived just a mile from her home, and she often walked down to visit me, carrying her denim bag full of magazines or interesting newspaper items that she thought I might wish to share with her. We talked about the articles and poems she had written and had been accepted by different publications. I told her of my desire to write and she encouraged me to do so. It was on her typewriter that I wrote my first article and she was the first person I called when my acceptance check came in the mail.

The home where she lived was the one she was born in and no other palace would have been so right for her. The combination of the old furniture with some of the new conveniences made a haven for many troubled persons who came to share their burdens with her. And receive some of her well-founded advice or sympathetic understanding. Her shoulders were *broad and her heart very large; so, no one came away without feeling better for the visit.*

After the death of her husband, she continued as before keeping busy with her various activities and growing family. The House was always busy with grandchildren coming and going or friends from all over coming to call. Her correspondence was almost a full-time job in itself. She had letters from all over the United States and she answered every one diligently.

I dreaded the first Christmas after the death of my husband. I knew it would be a lonely one for all of us, but Aunt Agnes came to the rescue by inviting us up there to share the day with her family. The house was full, the food was magnificent and the laughter flowed easily. Long before we were ready the day was over and it had been most pleasant for all of us.

In the later years when she became quite house bound from arthritis, she spent hours playing Scrabble with friends and relatives. It was difficult to ever win a game from her because of her quick mind and knowledge of words. She continued her writing, and until the last few months she had written a weekly column for a newspaper for several years.

Since I moved to Firth many of our visits have been on the telephone, but I have spent many pleasant afternoons at her home talking over the affairs of the day and sharing articles or books. I have been flattered and amused to have her call me her Geritol and often she has called to tell me that she was a little low in spirit and that I should make a trip out to bring her some Geritol. I was always glad to oblige whenever possible because I felt that she had given me so much herself.

In just one month from the time of her death she would have been 90 years old. Her life has touched many lives in that long span. She leaves a large, lonely family and hundreds of friends to mourn her passing, but she had a good life, and I doubt if there were many things she would have changed had she been given the opportunity. Always an optimist she greeted each new day with open arms and she enjoyed whatever it brought to the fullest. She will be missed greatly, but she left a heritage for all of us to profit by.

Men all grown with families of their own

(Alma wrote) *Land in the hills homesteaded by Justs was bought by Wally, Doug and Dad. They bought out Vin and traded for land down here at the home place.*

(Gwen wrote) *Jim Just had a sick spell and wanted to make sure if something happened to him, he would leave this earth without debt. He then sold a lot of land in the hills for pennies an acre.*

Jim Just and Bob Reid expanded their mountain holdings by buying out homesteaders in the Beaver Creek Field. Some they bought together, others only Jim purchased. They also owned a lot of ground from there up to Grave Creek, including the Wells' dry farm which had been farmed but had been about worthless for years. Jim decided to sell his acres there and came to see Bob and Agnes to talk about it. A Mr. Hogue wanted to buy it.

Mimi and Bob decided this would be a way to pay off the $8,000 mortgage they had taken out to purchase the Bennett kids' property in the Lower Field. Jack, Mabel and Bear wanted to go to California and they did so with this money. The ground was sold and the mortgage paid off.

Right away the dry farming came on strong again. Jim Just was sad that they had sold the ground too cheap. Jim Just decided to sell his interest in the Beaver Creek Field to Fred.

Mimi and Grandy needed some ready cash. They knew Gam had money from the dam payout of Horse Island, land that was covered when the American Falls Dam was constructed. Grandy and some boys went to the hills to get him, where he was at his homestead in the hills. They got stranded in the vehicle coming down the "W" above Wolverine. They had to get someone to help them with a team of horses. Mimi worried about them until they arrived the next morning.

(Alma wrote) *When we were married El and Jerrie were living at Lavaside, Gwen and Vin at the Charlie Just, Fred Twitchell place. Fred, Vin, and the boys all worked together on the home place and Vin's place. Hay, grain and sugar beets were grown then. Interest was mostly cattle for Fred, spuds and beets for Vin, cowboying for Wallace, and chickens and eggs for Doug.*

The Reids had a nice car, a Plymouth. Bob and Agnes had some sheep and some cattle. No regular wages were paid anyone. Fred was furnished hay and pasture for his cattle and Mimi would give him a beet check sometimes. Everything was either hand or horse labor.

Beets were thinned, weeded, watered, and topped by hand and then tossed into the wagon that hauled them to the beet dump. That of course was pulled by horses. Bob Reid had asthma that kept him down most of the time, although he would get on his big horse Sandy and check on things sometimes.

During these first years that Mom and Dad were married, the Just Reunion was started up again. (Doug said it was mostly Alma's idea). They had stopped celebrating in Emma's last years.

(Agnes wrote) *Yes, I am happy with my name, but no one else ever was. I never heard my husband use it except when I was in the next room. Our second son called me "Mimi" so that became official and my husband coached the grandchildren so that I have never been grandma. They don't know what to answer when someone asks about grandmother.*

(Mimi wrote about reading her verses at Alpine camp) *I don't know just how long I had been reading my verses, when I looked down the aisle, and there was my little Janene crossing over to find a seat. I'd already told my listeners that I couldn't see beyond the third row, but I could see her about nine or ten rows away. Then I looked a little to the left and found Fred and Alma and Rich and Donna and Merle and baby Becky. I think I must have gotten a very strange look on my face, for right during my reading, I said "my family just came in." I read a few more numbers and there came trooping in, Vin and Gwen and Wallace and Marlene and Doug and Bob. Then came Ted and Paul and Bill and little Gerry and Ginger then Debbie and Casey. I don't know in just what order they came, all I know is that it was surely a big bit of heaven for me. Such a handsome family and all of 'm, mine!*

(Mimi wrote) *I've been to the mailbox, to Marlene's twice and to Alma's three or four times today.*

(Mimi wrote in 1965) *I was telling Alma about Rich. I said, "I know it's none of my business what Rich does. I don't blame him if he's mad at me." Then Alma said, "Of course it's your business. I hope you're here to help raise them all." What a good message to a mother-in-law!!*

Barbara Reid Hanson described Mimi this way. "A mother, writer, homemaker, cook and babysitter all wrapped into a vivacious little "Mimi" as her 20 grandchildren call her. Oh! How lucky I am to be one of them."

My Dad loved to give people nicknames. Wallace had the most given by Fred. *Punch* because he was a cowpuncher, and *Willis* because it sounded like Wally. This morphed into *Willis Hanson* since there was a real Willis Hanson.

Ma Reid was Marlene. (Frank Pratt called his wife Ma Pratt). Wallace started calling Molly, Ma Reid, and it was funny because she was such a cute little thing. I hope Molly thought so too.

"The Old-Timer" was Dad's nickname for Doug when they both got older.

"Torpedo Neck" was Dad's nickname for Vin, but he has no idea where it came from. "Pendle" Dad's nickname for Gwen, same way, didn't know where it came from. In later years he called her "Gweny."

After Grandy died Mimi distributed her cattle to her sons. She had 40 or 50 head. They could have their pick of the cattle starting with El, then Vin, Fred, Doug and Wallace, then up the line from Wallace to El and back down until they were gone. Vin knew some names of the cattle he got. They remembered El saying, "Should I pick her? Should I pick her?" trying to get them to hurry with their choice. What a simple, fair way for distribution.

(Gwen wrote) *Mimi loved it when a grandchild would ask "Mimi do you have any gingerbread?" If she was temporarily out, given a few minutes a fresh pan would miraculously appear.* Warm gingerbread was such a treat. Mimi's house and gingerbread will always be connected in my mind. There was a pan on the red stove countless times as we would bring in the mail on our way home from the bus stop.

(Mimi wrote) *Mother's Day 1956, Jerry, Gwen and I were discussing Reid men down at Gwen's. We all agreed that Reid men do not like to be told what to do. They'd rather do things without being told. Jerry said, "You don't need to worry about anybody bossing Doug. A Reid can't be bossed."*

I was telling Alma about it and she said it might be somewhat true that they didn't like to be bossed. Then she added: "But even if they don't like to take orders, they certainly <u>never give any</u>."

(Mimi wrote in 1965) *We have a new card game "Hard Nose" pinochle and even Fred and Wallace like to play.*

...That's why I love my daughter-in-laws. They love my sons. If I found one of them not loving my son, then I'd have reason to complain.

Wally, Vin and Fred were at a banquet. A fellow wondered if they were brothers and commented that they had the same ears. He reconsidered what he said and thought it may have been taken as an insult. "Oh, don't get me wrong, they're beautiful ears!"

(Gwen wrote) *Mimi is almost synonymous with "Scrabble," a board word game. Any visitor could be challenged to a game and more often than not be beaten.* Gwen, Alma and Marlene were often her partners. Her niece, Clarice, often came 2 or 3 afternoons a week. (Mimi wrote) *Sometimes Clarice and I play ten games by working late.*

Dad told about a hamburger stand they had at the Eastern Idaho State Fair one year. He thinks Doug was the instigator at about 15. Mom, Silva Burrus, Phyllis, Grandy and Doug were the workers. (Isn't that a strange crew?) One time an Indian came back and told Alma she had forgotten to put the hamburger in the bun. I guess the money was good, Mom said she came home with her pockets full of bills.

We took Wally, Vin, Doug and Fred to the old house to tell us memories. Wally said that he had a drawer in the Post Office desk that he used for his treasures. He walked over and opened it. Sure enough, inside were his match book collection, some high school name cards, and a map he had drawn as a kid. It was papers taped together of fields, the river winding through them, and animals in corrals. The fences were all drawn like kids do, appearing like they're lying flat on the ground. "Those spider looking things are cows," he said.

Tracy Hawker was El's hired man for years and told us about Eldro's struggle between honoring his wife and doing what he thought was right. He missed out on so many visits and laughter with our family.

(Gwen wrote) *Eldro was so patient, so kind, so loving it really hurt us all when he was in bad shape walking or having teeth problems but one day Fred called him and said, "Butch I'm coming to get you today and we are going to the hills." He was told he had to be home at a certain time (And he was). Alma, Fred's wife, took a picture of him with Vin and Fred before they left, and the three of them spent the whole day in the hills and listened to Eldro's remembrances of his early days. It had been 40 years since he had been in his beloved hills. He still had some heifers and was meeting the veterinary to do something with them the morning he died. Believe me, Heaven is a better place because Eldro is there.*

Fred, Eldro, Vin in their customary chambray denim shirts

One time Fred and Vin went to a horsedrawn machinery show. They knew Eldro loved teams and wished he was there to enjoy the outing. They bought a model cast iron team and machine to give him, but he died before they could give him the gift.

(Mimi wrote about pinochle) *Doug gets mad at me for bidding too much and too often.*

(Mimi wrote*) Being the mother of 5 tall sons I know that every one of them is more Reid than Just and I rejoice it is so.*

(Mimi wrote about a Mother's Day) *I got to see all my sons and about half of the grandchildren.*

(Mimi wrote) *Children are an investment, grand-children are the dividends.*

When our folks got elderly, Wallace had the idea for all the brothers and wives to go to lunch in town the first Sunday of each month. He said he had the idea when Eldro was still alive and wished he had pushed for it then. They, Vin and Gwen, Wallace and Marlene, Fred and Alma, and Doug kept the tradition for several years. The lunches stopped for a time after Vin died, but our sis Janene (our parents' caregiver) started it up again.

After Dad had his throat surgery, when he needed a good excuse to refuse something (especially pinochle) he would say, "*I can't play pinochle good since my surgery.*" We girls always laughed of course.

Mom and Dad and Vin and Gwen were on a road trip. Dad and Vin were in the front seat and went by a nightclub. Vin saw the sign and said, "Look Fred it says, 'LIVE GIRLS! GIRLS! GIRLS!" From the back seat, Gwen piped up, "We're live girls!" to which Vin replied, "Yes, but, you've been alive for so long!"

(Alma wrote) *I asked Fred what his description of a perfect housewife was (because I knew how he didn't like all the yard work I did) and he said as near as I can quote him – "One who not only really knows what to do with a shovel, but also makes delightful and highly nutritious meals always."* When I read this to them late in life, Dad said he would add to it now, "and doesn't stop cooking when she turns 80!"

(Alma wrote) *I had peanut butter and maple centers (*for her Christmas chocolates)*. I had Fred try them both so he could tell me which he liked best. He thought a little and then said: "Well, that's like making me choose between you and Reba!"* (Reba McEntire, Dad's favorite Country and Western singer)

Vin and Chick helped build the Fred Reid house in 1952. Vin said he helped build 3 houses for Fred. He roofed the white house when Fred and Alma moved in and helped rebuild our house after it burned in 1969.

This shows Doug perfectly. (Doug wrote to Kit) *Speaking of saving pennies, I saved a five-cent stamp today, but had a big job doing it. It was on one of Marlene's letters from Bill Pettite and when she wasn't looking, I peeled it off the envelope. (It's the stamp on this letter. If you want to look at it) but the blamed thing had been torn in two in the first place, so naturally it was still in two pieces when I stole it. Well, I started home with it (or them). When I got out to the road, I couldn't find it (them) so I went back looking for it. (I mean them) in the snow and clear back to their garage. Couldn't find it (them) and decided I must have put it in some of my pockets, so I'd look some more when I got home. I did. No trace of them. Well, I forgot about them for a while, but in the afternoon, I went back up, and found them both where I'd dropped them on the garage floor. This time I put them in my shirt pocket, and promptly forgot them. Several hours later when I did remember them, I only had one piece of it left in my pocket. I thought sure I had been permanently foiled that time, but I remembered I had wiped up some water from the floor with a Kleenex I had had in my shirt pocket. A quick scanning of the floor revealed the missing part, and I finally got them stuck to stay on this envelope. Now if the black faced buck just doesn't recognize it as the one that came through uncancelled in today's mail, I've committed the perfect crime (if Marlene doesn't miss it!!!)*

Neighbors, Friends, and Origins of Reid Sayings

Wilber and Nelle Vincent were lifelong friends of the Reids. Their son Dwain and Vin were pals, and sometimes Dwain would stay at the Reid home. (Mimi wrote in a letter to Nelle in 1931) *We miss Dwain. Really should not for there are ten of us, but then, not any of us are Dwain. Jerrie and El are here right now to help with the haying, we've had Kit's boy nearly a month, and we have a big Scotchman, who can just get in the door and makes Rufus look like a little boy, so I really cannot complain of being either lonesome or idle.*

(Mimi wrote) *If we had boys hanging on the branches of every tree there would still be room for Dwain.*

1929 (Mimi wrote after the Vincents moved to Utah and they wanted Vin to go to high school with their son Dwaine) *You are certainly nice people to offer to take our Vin, but we have not been able to arrive at any decision. It only took Rufus about thirty seconds to decide that he did not want him to go and I am more fully convinced than ever that I am not made of the stuff my mother was, for he is just the age that I was when I went away to school and she had no other girls left, while I have a lot of other boys, still only one Vin. I feel that he is really the one who should make the decision, but all he will say is that he does not have to decide right away.*

This picture was probably taken soon after Fred's 10th birthday when he received the $10 Stetson. Here he wears Mimi's buckskin gloves and the Angora chaps given to Vin from Wilbur and Nelle Vincent.

Henry and Margaret Burrells Williams lived in the Presto Burrell home. They had lots of girls and 2 boys. Hank was Fred's age and was a very close friend and playmate. Margaret and Henry were close couple friends to Grandy and Mimi. Dolly Williams and husband Walt Tschikof and Grace Williams were the closest to the Reid family.

Dad told me of one time he went into the milk barn ahead of Hank and acted like he was getting mugged. Hank was smaller and younger than Dad, but he ran in to help him.

This is the same $10 Stetson. It lasted many years, even after El yanked it down on his head and took a handful of the brim off, as evident in the picture.

Dad remembered the yearly creamery picnics. Uncle Henry (Williams) hauled milk to the creamery and he invited the Reids to be his guests at these functions.

1942 (Mimi wrote) *Margaret Williams stayed while her daughter thinned beets with the boys. The second week I had to go to Rufus and she was here to mother my boys and take care of the house. I went to Pocatello expecting to be back in a few hours and I stayed six days, but I never gave a thought to things at home. She even had to bear the news to the poor boys that their daddy might not come back. It was a terrible thing for her to have to do, but I knew they must be prepared for the worst. She stayed until we brought Rufus home.*

Minerva Kohlhepp Teichert was a local historian and noted author of *Drowned Memories*. She was also a painter, known for her depictions of western scenes with religious themes. Many of the Mormon temples have her paintings of pioneer and Mormon events. She gave a picture of magpies to Agnes. Fred remembered it hung in the kitchen for a time.

Minerva is my husband Jack Clark's great aunt. My mother-in-law gave me a print of Minerva's of magpies. When I found a magpie picture in the attic of the old Just home, a signed original, I knew immediately it was hers. It was painted in 1924 and is signed M Teichert like she did in her early works. Later she signed with Minerva Teichert.

Minerva was very outspoken about her religion, and Mimi wasn't religious of any organized faith, so the friendship wasn't close. After 30 years El took Mimi to Cokeville where Minerva lived. It was an unexpected visit, but when Mimi got out of the car, Minerva called out to her, "Agnes!"

Neal Sage married **Madge Stull** the same day that Grandy and Mimi were married. The Sages had been friends of the Justs, and Neal was in the banking business with Nels. He later went to prison for a time for embezzlement.

Robert's cousin, **Maudie Lockyer Wring,** a daughter of Kate and Mayford Lockyer, lived at the intersection of Presto and Firth-Wapello Rd. She had a wild bunch of boys that would wire their boots to the stirrups of their saddles. "They could ride awful rank horses that way," said Fred.

Mimi and **Mama Cook**, (mother of Darrel and Glenn) were at a church function. Mrs. Cook got home without her purse and called Mimi to ask if she had taken it home by mistake. Mimi went straight to the church and found it where it had fallen out of sight. She took it to Mrs. Cook, but wondered if she thought she had taken it, and since she was confronted, brought it back. It was a situation that Mimi never felt was resolved and felt uncomfortable ever after with Mama Cook.

(Mimi wrote a letter to Glenn Cook) *I have often thought I'd like to come see you and Emma and find out what is causing the unpleasantness between the Cooks and Reids. Surely intelligent, grown-up people should be able to get along, what is the matter with us all?*

Glenn Cook lived in the old Presto Burrell home. Fred said Glen wouldn't clean out the cattle guard so his pigs would find their way to the Reids and cause havoc. Dad once roped a big pig and lead him back home.

"Gotta go ….. so," was attributed to Glenn Cook.

One time when a mare on the team had a colt, Glenn observed, "Colts, guess that's something not worth raising."

"Guess there's been a lot of people die," Glenn Cook said. One-time Vin and Gwen were on a long road trip. After many miles of silence, they were passing a grave yard. They looked at each other and said in unison, "Guess there's been a lot of people die."

When it took a lot of seed to plant a field, Glenn Cook said "Ground sure holds it."

The Reids had a neighbor named **Richard Dye**. I don't know any stories about this man but he is the one that is responsible for the "Richard" name being used in the family. Dad said he was a good guy.

John A Jorgensen was a neighbor right across the river on the Reservation where Dad leased property from the Indians. We always called him "John A." He called my Dad, Fret. His wife was Beaver Dick's grand-daughter, Vera. She divorced John A, married his brother, then finally took off with the hired man, Johnny Baldwin.

Dad told of going to John A's house in Shelley. John proudly shared some pickled herring he got from his native Sweden. It was smelly and Dad couldn't even think of eating it. He snuck it in his pocket when John wasn't looking.

Fred bought the John A place and got his equipment in the deal. There was an International M and H (Super M), a beet topper, a grain drill, a mower, a farm hand, a plow, rakes and a harrow. The total for the equipment was $9,000 to add to the $28,000 for the 68 acres of land. My brother Rich and his wife Charlotte built their home on the property.

There are only a few isolated parcels on the Reservation owned by non-Indians. Rich told me the Tribe needed money to finish the Fort Hall Irrigation project and sold some land to the whites. The land was first purchased by Emmett Morris, who sold to John A. Jorgensen, who sold to Fred Reid and is now operated by my brother Rich Reid.

Ann Hansen Hayes was a lifelong friend of Mimi's from Albion school days. She wrote of Agnes, *"One need not see her come to feel her presence."* She entered our family tree when Vin's son, Bob, married Christy Crockett. Ann was Christy's grandmother Carrie's sister.

The **Eastern Idaho Grazing Association**, an agricultural cooperative, was founded in 1916 to purchase land and secure grazing leases for 73 original charter members including Emma Just, Fred Bennett and Robert Reid. There are still many Reid descendants that summer their cattle on the Association.

The Hayes family were Mimi's good friends. There were two brothers and their wives, Cliff and Becky, and Tim and Elva. Tim had a printing press and Elva had a gift shop in the same building, right next to the Corner Café in Blackfoot. Cliff was a mortician and Becky was a singer and gave piano lessons. Dad said she would play the organ at their house and it was really fun. These couples would be invited out to the earliest spring party at the Reids, a picnic close to the river named The Frog Festival.

Billy Stoddard owned land along Beaver Creek. He lived in a cabin during the summers and worked with the Reids who ran cattle with Jim Just and Billy. He was a very short man and the roof was appropriately low. The Reid men would stay overnight sometimes if they were up working cattle. I don't know how the Lanky Reids could be in that cabin. Billy Stoddard had big thoroughbred horses and was always bragging them up. One time Dad asked "out of the top 10 best horses in Idaho that ever lived, how many do you think you've owned?" Billy answered seriously "6 or 7." "Oh Geeeamsh!" a Billy Stoddard saying, was used as an exclamation meaning "Oh Gosh!"

Agnes Cutler was the nurse and wife of Dr. Cutler, and attended all 5 Reid baby births. She was born in Utah and married a William Cutler who died of small pox while on a mission in Pennsylvania. She had a son while he was gone. She was making a dress for William's homecoming when her father came to tell her of his passing. She took her son and went to Salt Lake to take a nursing class and was in the first graduation class. It was here she met and married A. E. Cutler, her late husband's cousin. They moved to Shelley and started doctoring in the town and rural areas. Agnes lived to a ripe old age; one clipping Gwen had was a tribute on her 105th birthday.

Berkley and Florence Larsen were neighbors, friends and work partners. Florence was from the city and had nothing to do with the farm/ranch. Their children were Jerrie (married Eldro), Maxine (Nina Jower's mother), Naida, Allan (Bus), Berkley (Bim), and Reid. Gwen surmised they thought they were better than the Reids because they were Mormons, even though they really liked them.

Dad, Bus and Bim were around 10 years old when the Larsens had a relative living in the bunkhouse working for them. The Larsen kids knew about a gun that this older kid (about 20-25) had and wanted him to show it to Dad. It was a strange gun, a "four shooter." This kid handed Dad the gun and it immediately went off. They were all standing in a tight circle, and the bullet luckily went straight in the air and into a porch support post. Horrified and scared, they vowed never to tell. That lasted a good 50 years. Dad knows he hardly touched it, surely the kid didn't know it was loaded, and it must have had a hair trigger.

Berkley Larsen said "Oh yes, the Reids always have time to brew coffee!" This is true. There was a huge enamel coffee pot just suited for the purpose, but in later years, often working out of doors, they would brew it in an empty coffee can the old-fashioned way. Put coffee on the top of cold water, bring to a boil so the grounds turned over. Take it off the fire (sometimes with a pair of vice grips) and dribble some cold water in it to settle the grounds.

Allan Larsen (Bus) and J Berkeley Larsen (Bim) were brothers. **Jim Just** called them "Biss and Bum."

Grandy and Mimi were going to a church function with Berkley and Florence. Berkley was driving (unknown if it was horses or a car). Berkley was driving faster than Grandy was comfortable with and he told him so. Berkley said they were late for church to which Grandy replied, "I'd rather be 10 minutes late for church than 15 minutes early to hell."

Allen (Bus) was quoted *"Through all my childhood and college years, I never had a better friend than Fred Reid."*

(Mimi wrote in 1947) *Barbara Larsen (married to Bus Larsen) was visiting Gwen today and she said she hoped her boys would grow up to be just like the Reid boys.*

Western author **B.M. Bower** and Mimi corresponded, and spent a long vacation together on the ranch. B.M. took a buggy up the Blackfoot River (Mimi may or may not have been with her) to see Daphne Jemmett and get some material for her book. The book Ranch on the Wolverine was written after her visit to the area. There is a place in the book where the cowboy is cleaning the cabin by dumping a bucket of water on the floor, scrubbing the corners and then sloshing it out the door. Daphne was doing the same when B.M. visited.

B.M. Bower on Monte   Agnes on Sid

This was written about Bower's visit:

During the summer of 1913, the noted writer of western books B. M. Bower spent two months as a guest of the Reid Family. While there she found the setting for her story "Ranch on the Wolverine." Her novels ranked with Zane Grey's. Few people knew that B.M. (Bertha Muzzy) was a woman. She contended that western books would have more public appeal if they appeared that they were authored by a man. She was a very good friend of Montana's great artist, Charles M Russell. She was given several of his original, now famous pictures.

(Mimi wrote) *She brought her own saddle and outfit. She even brought a Charlie Russell original that hung on our wall and a bed sized Serape* (hand-woven, colorful, southwestern shawl) *on our bed.*

I found in the History of the War Bonnet Round-up 1911-1967:

She and Agnes Reid, both being avid horsewomen spent many days riding throughout the valley. They often rode into Blackfoot and back the same day, a distance of fifteen miles. They estimated they had ridden four hundred miles during the two months Bower spent at the Reid ranch. In September, 1913, the main topic discussed was the forthcoming War Bonnet Round-up. The celebrated author persuaded her friend Agnes to join her in entering the women's saddle horserace. The day before the race was to take place they rode their twelve-year-old ranch horses the eighteen miles to Idaho Falls, accompanied by Mr. Reid. They spent the night as guests of Kate Johnson, daughter of Charles Tautphaus, the man who planned the local park were the round-up was held.

Mrs. Reid's account of the race follows---------"Bower wanted to ride in the race for the sensation of it. Dressed in our long-divided skirts of corduroy, so the wind would not blow them and show our ankles, we raced our fat, old cattle horses around the track far behind the professionals. But we got our sensation and the dust."

When Kent Just told **Clarice Mattson**, he was going to auctioneer school she said, "Finally, a Just will get paid for talking!"

Mom and Dad were at the State Fair and ran into **Jim Mattson**. He asked if they had seen his mother. They answered no. "*Well, have you heard her then?*" Clarice was a loud talker.

Jim Mattson got his high school diploma the same time as Fred in a ceremony for WWII veterans that were at war and couldn't graduate with their classmates. June said she was glad that Jim had his high school diploma, now he could get a good paying job.

The "Bennett Brats" (**Jack and Bear**) wired the door to the shop so anyone opening it would get shocked.

George Metz, was an Indian friend. He said about his kids "*I don't think they're going to amount to much.*" Dad would use this phrase often, usually when anything went wrong on the ranch, "*I don't think we're going to amount to much.*"

"*When is he ever gonna die?!*" George Metz said about John A to Dad. It's a favorite phrase as well, making light of a very serious topic!

Dad's lifelong friend **Allan Thompson** was an army buddy and lived nearby in Shelley.

(Mimi wrote) *The other day your folks were away and Allan Thompson came to see me. What a visit we had. He looks fine. Better than he has in years and of course we were both very happy. Then we talked about a lot of things and finally I said: 'Allan, I've always wanted to tell you how much I appreciated it that you told your people in the Mormon church that if they wanted someone as a pattern for fine manhood just look at Fred Reid.' He answered right fast 'and I meant every word of it.' It was a good visit and since it happened so long ago I wondered if you had ever heard that Allan did make a talk in church or mutual soon after they came back from Georgia, and said the nicest things about your dad. It has been a wonderful friendship even better because it was Mormon and non-Mormon. It proves that gold is where you find it and good folks are where they are.*

Frank Pratt was a good friend and neighbor of the Reids, and a wonderful old-time cowboy. I remember him standing, visiting with my dad and slapping his buckskin gloves to his other hand. He loved to drive around the community visiting with whoever was home, including the Mrs. of the household.

One time Harold Twitchell was riding on the Fort Hall Bottoms with Frank, who was the Reservation range rider at the time. Frank called him over and said, "Kid, if you see a saddle horn sticking out of the bog, don't ride there." The Bottoms are a boggy mess and I know from experience you have to know where it's safe to ride.

Frank Pratt is quoted as saying, "Looks like she'd learn!" Or "he'd learn" or "they'd learn."

He would say when they were having a bad time driving cattle in the summer, "Looks like grown men would know better than to drive cattle up a hill in the heat of the day!"

The Reid boys often quoted Frank by saying, "Everything has to be jist." meaning just right.

Frank Pratt said after a cold day of riding. "If I live to be a hundred, I'll never learn to put on enough clothes!" This when he was way underdressed, wearing a short Levi jacket or "jumper" as it was called.

Frank Pratt said when a cow was dying its eyes are "green and glassy."

If we're riding in a pickup and need to take our coat off because we're too hot, we're "doing an old Frank Pratt."

My sister Wendy and her husband Mark Pratt bought the old Frank Pratt place (The Polegate Ranch) from Leslie and Beatrice Cooper. Beatrice was Frank's daughter.

Richard Hughes (Dick) was married to Sarah Pratt and had children, Ronald and Bob among others. Ronald's daughter Charlotte married my brother Rich.

Grandy was getting treatments for his asthma in Portland. Ronald Hughes was stationed there during WWII. They met unexpectedly on the street and these homesick friends were overjoyed to see each other.

Dick is credited with saying, "Looks like it's going to be a late spring, it always is." And this, describing his crop of grain, "It's thin and short, but the heads is small." My brother Rich loves to use this one!

Ronald Hughes complimented the cook by exclaiming, "Looks like you had pretty good luck with that."

Bob Hughes was heard to say, "Those Reids are the weirdest bunch I've ever seen!"

My Dad and his brothers used, "that was pretty" a lot. It describes a mistake big or small. Unknown origin.

Everett Lyon, Dorothy Phillips' husband (Clarice), claimed "it doesn't take as much water as some people think." (to make good coffee)

When the beets were in need of thinning or harvesting one fellow, **Al Butram**, would come back year after year. He lived out west of Idaho Falls in the sagebrush and rocks with an Indian lady. He was alerted that he and his buddies had a job waiting for them. Bob and Agnes would furnish them with groceries, or feed them in the house. They would stay in the homestead cabin or the little shack by the lower field depending where the work was closest.

Pratt is an old word that means butt or bottom. (for example pratt fall). Al Butram was introduced to Bud Pratt. Al laughed and commented. "You have an even worse name than mine!"

Gordon Prouse told someone, "Fred Reid isn't too bad of a guy if you can catch him sober." That made us kids laugh because our Dad was a teetotaler.

Dad said that Mr. Prouse told of a cow that died. He "saw it the night before and it was standing there fine. The next morning it was dead. He said that he figured that it had died "sometime durrrrrin' the night." Durrin is said slow and deliberate.

The **Johnson Brothers** had a nice ranch on the river. They were doing something in their cattle operation and it was working like a charm. Someone asked them if they were going to do it again next year, they exclaimed in surprise, "Oh, no . . !"

"That's ourn" was an expression Kenny Johnson used meaning "me too." Dad had taken in some weaners to sell, and Kenny said, "That's ourn." Dad used the term a lot.

Critters

Grandy and his boys on Banjo

Blanche Pratt wrote a nice tribute in the Bingham County book to Banjo. He was a dependable horse for the teachers to ride to school, and to Firth for weekends home. Children learned to ride on him. Banjo died at the age of 31 on July 4 th in Vin's pasture.

Grandy's last horse was named Sandy. When Wally grew old, he named a horse Sandy for his last horse.

There was a horse that appeared at the Reid Ranch when dad was a boy. They named him 'Stray.' He was "the best horse that ever lived," a good kid's horse and great man's working cow horse. Jack Anderson (Indian neighbor) finally laid claim to him so Bob Reid bought him back. This story is like our "Lady Bird" horse that appeared when we were kids. She was a single footer and great fun to ride, much faster than our regulars, Sally and Burt. Dad thought she was ugly, a tall thoroughbred looking bay. We finally found out that the sheepherder from Allan Thompson's sheep camp on the Presto Bench had lost her. Allan gave her to us when he found out how much we liked her.

Doug named horses "long faces." We never saw Doug on a horse. He is the only one of the Reids that felt like Nels about horses. Dad would catch the horses from the far reaches of the ranch and put them in the corral so we could ride them. We always figured it was Doug that let them out again.

(Mimi wrote) *Little Joe Adams (Chet Adam's grandad) came up on horseback. Joe had such a dandy horse, etc., everything completed so I made him stay with Rufus and take care of the baby while I rode his outfit up to Burrell's with the girls. My, it was fun! I just wished there was looking glasses all the way along the road so I could see how smart I looked.*

Dad told of pasturing horses during the summer on what became the old Frank Pratt place. Jim Just had the land and they had a bunch of mares and a stallion owned by someone else to breed them. There was an old homestead and a cistern close to the doorway. The horses would go into the house to shade up in the heat of the day. When someone went to check on the horses, they found five or six horses had fallen in the cistern and died and a colt was walking around on the bodies.

Mimi rode Sandy to visit the Williams family because she was snowed in. They lived north of Firth - you had to go over the railroad tracks, and across the highway. She had left their house and was about to cross the highway when the train whistle blew and spooked the horse, he ran away along the highway towards Shelley. Mimi was scared he would run into traffic or across the tracks, where he had crossed before. He ran on the highway, slipped and fell. She didn't break any bones but it took a long time for her to heal.

Turk (Sally's colt), was born when Dad was in Georgia. Wally was heading for high school in the car, hit the colt and broke its leg. Robert was very sick but was carried to the barn to bandage the colt's leg and it healed well. (We found a story that Mimi wrote about this) There was always a bump on his leg, but it didn't seem to bother him at all. We older kids rode Turk. He ate a potato that Doug had thrown over the fence, choked and died many years later. I barely remember getting off the school bus and hearing the sad news.

Fred, 27, on Turk, Wally, 17, on Belcher. Both horses were named for Fred's army buddies.

The Reids have always been ranchers and farmers. My Dad always ran a few cows for Doug, not individuals, but he would get a check for a percentage of the herd at sale time. I remember Doug going with Dad to feed the heifers many mornings. He would toss hay off the pickup, his long gray hair blowing in the wind.

Fred said from the day they were born, cattle (or horses or sheep) were always looking for some way to commit suicide.

Nels had a "T" brand that he bought from someone at Fort Hall and used it until he died. Grandy and Mimi continued to use it all their married lives. Fred used it until he forgot to renew it with the Brand Board in time and it was taken by someone else. Fred and Eldro took a trip to Boise to get brands. Fred got his TF brand that is the original T with an additional bar blending the two letters. Vin got a rafter V which is a V with a upside down V on top. Wallace had a lone pine. Cattle owned by their descendants still carry these brands.

Chief, Suz, Snip, Park, Mike, Pike, Star (Vin and Eldro) Queen, Jerrie, Beaut, Babe (Fred)

Nina, a niece of Jerrie and Eldro, gave the Reid men this neat picture. Dad remembered the horses and wrote their names below them. Fred is barely visible in back of Babe, note the hat and legs crossed in back of the horses' legs. He remembers there being 16 work horses at one time.

Horses liked to run away, there are lots of stories about these "runaways." One time while the thresher was being repaired, it was about noon so the men decided to eat before returning to the field. The machine was stopped facing a fence close to the house, but the 4-horse team was not tied up. The guys didn't get back to them quick enough and the horses took off, down along the fence and out through the gate and away to the West. Dad remembers it being quite a sight. The thresher was beat up and had to be repaired again, and the gate was in shambles. Dad didn't like to remember the mess.

Gam's team was named Fred and Sign. Dad thought the Sign name was Spanish.

Grandy had a favorite team, Jess and Bally; he could make them do anything. He was a great teamster. In a light moment, he joked that he "could drive a team where Nels couldn't drag a bridle!"

There was always a small bunch of sheep at the Reid's, maybe 60 head, mostly Mimi's. Molly had sheep before she was married, so they were her main love. We of this generation remember the fun of sheep shearing. The big wool bag was hung from the rafters in the back end of the Milk barn where the horse harnesses were hung. George Macanelly was the shearer. We kids would get inside the bag and stomp the wool down.

Fred had a team of goats when he was about 12. He traded Ford Ziegler two ducks and a worn-out leather lariat for them. El made the harness and Dad hitched them to a wagon that was on hand. They were named **Tom and Jerrie**. One was a castrated male and the other a female. The female was pregnant at the time but they didn't know it so he quickly had 3 goats. They weren't trained to pull when Dad got them, but soon got them to pull him around in the wagon. One time there was a community picnic down in the Grove. When they left the house, someone left the door open and the goats got in. They had their way, doing what goats do, then jumped out the kitchen window. Dad thinks maybe two windows were broken. I asked Doug if they ate the flowers, or how did they keep them out of the garden. He answered that they took them to "Goat Island" in the nearby Blackfoot River in the spring. The island doesn't exist now because the channel filled in, but this worked to keep them contained as they didn't want to cross the water. They lived a long life there, mostly, as Dad said, "wandering around."

The Reids regularly raised pigs for meat. Dad said baby pigs are the cutest animals ever. Grandy smoked the hams and bacon.

(Mimi wrote) *Dougie is just now establishing in the chicken business and takes such an interest in it. The first time I have really felt that he might be something like the other boys. He thrills over every egg and insists that I wake him at six thirty so he can have plenty of time to take care of his chickens. He is in the eighth grade.*

...Dougie has three hundred little chickens, three weeks old so there will be fried chicken when you make your annual visit. He has only lost six so he still has the 300 and he is a very pleased little boy.

Robert had geese. I remember finding goose nests, also being chased up a fence by honking, flapping geese and screaming for help until Dad came to rescue me. These must have been their descendants.

Dad said they had ducks. They didn't cook the eggs for breakfast, but used them in recipes sometimes.

One summer when the wood ticks were so bad Chick Just and Eldro Reid were fixing fence in the hills. When they came home, they were covered with ticks. Chick won the tally with over 50 for one day, and El was a close second.

Machinery and Vehicles

Nels thought a dam could be constructed on the Blackfoot River to generate hydroelectricity. The project was abandoned, we don't know why. It is near the mouth of the canyon below Wolverine Creek. The piles of rock can still be viewed from the bluff. Wally and Jim Mattson walked down to see the site in their later years and found a horse-drawn plow that must have been used in the dam building. This moment in history is notable to our family because one day Nels took Mimi with him to view the progress of the dam. It was the first time Mimi spotted Bob Reid who had a job helping with the excavation. She wrote later about how handsome he was.

Blackfoot River hydroelectric project
Robert is driving the team and his brother Donald is in left foreground

In 1935 Dad, Vin, and Robert went to Chicago by train to buy a Diamond T truck and a new Plymouth car. They were accompanied by three car dealers to bring other autos back to resell. The Indians were settling land on the Reservation and Grandy was paid $3,000 for some land he owned. He paid about $2,300 for both vehicles. They visited Glenn Pratt who was enrolled in a radio repair school, but when they stopped to visit, he decided he wanted to go home too. They had some time to kill in Chicago before the truck would be ready so they saw some sights, including the place where Dillinger was gunned down. There was a Chicago policeman that thought they were up to no good. Robert, Vin, Fred and Glenn Pratt surely didn't look suspicious?! He frisked Robert and felt the plastic toothbrush holder in his pocket. "What's this, a razor?" They picked up another Diamond T for the car dealership, so Vin and Glenn took one and Robert and Dad took the other. They went to Detroit to buy new Plymouths to lash to the back of the trucks to caravan home. They had to drive 35 miles per hour because they were new and that was how you broke them in. All the roads were paved but they were only two-lane. They were going through Wyoming when the cops stopped them. They were fined some outrageous fee for going across the state "without a permit to caravan." Robert objected and wanted to go into Laramie to discuss it with the authorities. The cop said "I'm the authority!" This put them low on funds, driving straight through the last 24 hours. No money for motels but dad knows they stopped to eat in Rock Springs. Robert was in okay health at that time.

Another memorable Diamond T story is the camping trip to Leadore to visit Chet Adams' parents and grandparents. Vin and Gwen, Eldro and Jerrie, Robert and Mimi, as well as Fred and the younger Reid boys all loaded up with bedding and food for all. Gwen remembers they took a lug of cherries.

Many years later, my brother Rich and cousin Ted vandalized the Diamond T truck as it was parked in the junk yard. Rich confessed, but the damage was done; broken out windows, etc. Dad saved the Diamond T metal name plate and it was displayed in their kitchen for many years.

El, Fred and Vin bought a threshing machine in 1936 from Mrs. Frank Hanny for $2,000 for their custom grain harvesting business. They used it on their own grain and others as far away as Bud Pratt and Frank Pratt and Wernette's. You would throw in the bundles of grain. Dad would hook it to the caterpillar to move it to another field. For a long time it was parked in the Lower Field along the ditch.

One-time Grandy and Jim Just bought a train car of wet beet pulp to feed to the cows. Using trucks, Grandy and Dad in one, El and Vin in another, they would get inside the train car and shovel pulp into the truck beds, haul it to the ranch and shovel it on to the pile they were making by the cattle. Then they would still have to shovel it into the mangers to feed the cows. Fred and Grandy's truck was probably a 1929 or 1930 Model D. Vin and El were heading back in an empty truck one trip and hit Johnny Baldwin's dog by the school and rolled the truck. It was a Model T Ford. It wasn't much good when they were hauling and less after it rolled.

Dad and Vin bought a 1926 Harley Davidson motorcycle around 1933. They had put up Jim Just's hay and with the profits bought it from a man in Blackfoot for 50 dollars. The only color Dad remembers is the green gas tank. but he was colorblind! The farthest they ever went was to see Jimmy Shikashio in Shelley. Dad remembers riding it to look over the Presto Bench and watching a big wind storm rage across the plowed fields in the valley below. The bike was in pretty bad shape when they got it, and while Dad was in the army the motor was removed by Milon Hutchinson to make an air compressor. Dad has always loved motorcycles and when Jack bought a Harley he was thrilled.

Dad remembers buying a new 2-ton truck, probably the '49 Studebaker we remember, for $3,283.27. They hauled in a load of fat steers, which sold for enough to buy the truck.

Burial Sites

Isabelle Reid ----Robin Cemetery off the Arimo exit, opposite side of the freeway
James Reid ---American Falls Cemetery
Donald (Don) Reid---American Falls Cemetery
Andrew Goodenough ----Harkness Cemetery, McCammon (unmarked)
Mary Bell Goodenough ------ Harkness Cemetery, McCammon (unmarked)
Millie Reid ----Springfield-Sterling Cemetery
Richard Reid (Dick) ---Springfield-Sterling Cemetery
William (Bill) Reid---Springfield-Sterling Cemetery
Kittie Reid Blair, Ed Blair and Kathleen----Firth Cemetery
Jim Reid--------Firth Cemetery
Eldro and Jerrie Reid and son Eldro Jay Reid-------Goshen Cemetery
Agnes Just Reid, Robert Reid and Doug Reid ------Goshen Cemetery
Wallace and Marlene Reid, son Cliff Reid-----Goshen Cemetery
Fred Reid and Alma Jemmett Reid----------Hillcrest Cemetery, Shelley
Vin and Gwen Davis Reid----------ashes spread in Reid valley

Epilogue

I am sure this isn't all correct, but it is my best effort.

If I could give you a bit of advice, it would be to ask questions of your living ancestors. And keep adding to a notebook of what you have discovered. Someday, someone is going to want to know and you will have the answer.

More information can be found at ancestry.com. I would like to encourage you to enter your information. It is a very fun hobby and makes our tree even richer. It is amazing how fast the tree can get outdated as marriages, babies and deaths occur.

A very rewarding hobby, it has provided me many hours of pleasure.

Special thanks to my sister Wendy Pratt for the editing; the book is much better than the rough copy I sent her. And my sister Becky. She reads the book over and over and still finds mistakes. I also want to thank Anna Pratt Lickley, Wendy and Mark Pratt's daughter, for arranging it in book form. Also thanks to Rick Just for publishing my work. I appreciate you all so much for your input.

Sources

Legal documents
Presto Press
Family Search LDS website
Idaho State Journal
Overland Pioneer travel, LDS website
Shelley Pioneer
Blackfoot News
Idaho History Bingham County book Volume I 1890- 1990
Idaho History Bingham County book Volume II 1895 -1995
Agnes Just Reid *Letters of Long Ago* 1923, 1973
ancestry.com
letters and writings found at Kittie Reid Blair's home
Agnes Just Reid diaries 1923 - 1976
Agnes Just Reid's correspondence and other writings
Alma Jemmett Reid, *Along the Rivers,* 1994
Snake River Echoes 1985
Pages of the Past
Pages of unknown source, that someone had copied
Drowned Memories, Minerva Teichert
History of the War Bonnet Round-up 1911-1967

www.ingramcontent.com/pod-product-compliance
Lightning Source LLC
Chambersburg PA
CBHW051511100526
44585CB00043B/2464